POETRY C(

GREAT MINDS

Your World...Your Future...YOUR WORDS

United In Poetry Vol II
Edited by Donna Samworth

 Young**Writers**

First published in Great Britain in 2005 by:
Young Writers
Remus House
Coltsfoot Drive
Peterborough
PE2 9JX
Telephone: 01733 890066
Website: www.youngwriters.co.uk

All Rights Reserved

© *Copyright Contributors 2005*

SB ISBN 1 84602 092 1

Foreword

This year, the Young Writers' 'Great Minds' competition proudly presents a showcase of the best poetic talent selected from over 40,000 up-and-coming writers nationwide.

Young Writers was established in 1991 to promote the reading and writing of poetry within schools and to the youth of today. Our books nurture and inspire confidence in the ability of young writers and provide a snapshot of poems written in schools and at home by budding poets of the future.

The thought, effort, imagination and hard work put into each poem impressed us all and the task of selecting poems was a difficult but nevertheless enjoyable experience.

We hope you are as pleased as we are with the final selection and that you and your family continue to be entertained with *Great Minds United In Poetry Vol II* for many years to come.

Contents

Siani Rahman (13)	1
Danni Walpole (12)	2
Samuel Landau (15)	3
Chantal Skett (13)	4
Aoibhinn Byrom (11)	5
Sasha Cox	5
Cheri Allcock (14)	6
Leah Ormerod (12)	7
Maxine Churcher (12)	8
Christopher Newman (16)	8
Nathan Smith (12)	9
Kerry McDaid	9
Ricky Leftly (13)	10
Salih Abdoun Mohammed (11)	10
Rachel Kennedy (15)	11
Chanelle Bryan (12)	11
Minakshi Neelam Samrai (14)	12
Belinda Forde (13)	12
Jacqueline van Zetten (15)	13
Sophie Falco (12)	13
Lorna-Marie Gilyeat (14)	14
Erin Maloney-Cox (8)	15
Jenny Wong (16)	16
Jonathan Cox (11)	17
Natalie Gibson (14)	18
Stacey Roberts (12)	18
Rishi Patel (13)	19
Kiran Perry & James Quirke (13)	19
Kaz Davies (16)	20
Terri Masters (14)	20
Lucy Laycock (15)	21
Sarah-Bayeya Nyemba (13)	21
Sam Mustafa (14)	22
Jenny Clark (11)	23
Tom Webb (13)	24
Amy Hawkins (13)	24
Emma Tarbuck (16)	25
Lauren Davidson (12)	25

Xanthe Batt (15)	26
Kirsty Wood (14)	26
Rebecca Wade (13)	27
Laura James (16)	28
Claire Komar (11)	29

Aberdour School, Tadworth
Ray Barron (12)	30
Andrew Phillips (12)	31
Alexander Gibbons (12)	32
Joshua Chan-Lok (12)	32
Gordon Shephard (13)	33
Mayuri Pattni (12)	34
Daniel Pearson (12)	34
Sam Freeman (13)	35
Stephen Hume (13)	35
Jonathan Matthews (13)	36
Christian Killoughery (12)	36
Shahail Woodcock (12)	37
Emma Diggins (13)	37
Thomas Pearson (13)	38

Alleynes High School, Stone
Kim Loughhead (15)	38
Roseanna Gray (15)	39

Babington House School, Chislehurst
Helena Oakes & Hannah Rickwood (12)	39
Nicola Jarman (12)	39
Lucie Bentley (12)	40
Casey Adams	40
Holly Barker (12)	40
Sûreya Ibrahim (12)	41
Latisha Elliott (13)	41
Sophie Walker (13)	41
Annabelle Tricks (12)	42
Emma Griffin Beat (12)	42
Lucy Colin	42

Brae High School, Shetland
Danielle Aitken (14)	43
Stewart Williamson (13)	43
Anya Charleson (14)	44
Leanne Shedden (14)	45
Thomas Wyeth (14)	46
Siân Bryant (14)	47

Berwickshire High School, Duns
Suzy Pope (17)	48

Cardiff High School, Cyncoed
Richard Roberts (14)	49
Andrew Drayton (14)	49
James Abbott (14)	49

Hayesfield School, Bath
Molly Shatwell (12)	50
Lucy Sullivan (12)	50
Hannah Woodland (11)	51
Esme Haughton (12)	51
Lizzie Thorn (11)	52
Libby Skinner (12)	52

High School of Dundee, Dundee
Roxanne O'Fee (14)	53
Rachael McLellan (12)	54
Rachel Jones (13)	55
Rachel Coleman (13)	56
Vanita Nathwani (12)	57
Eilidh Firth (14)	58
Josh Ivinson (12)	59
Annie Ning (14)	60
Kirsty McEwan (12)	61
Rachael Sinclair (13)	62
Victoria Sinclair Beat (14)	63
Shona Watson (14)	64
Poppy Drummond (14)	65
Caitlin McDonald (13)	66
Stuart Mires (13)	67

Rachel Fraser (14)	68
Katy Rodger (12)	69
Adam Robertson (13)	70
Rachel Clark (13)	71
Fabliha Hussain (12)	72
Erin Middleton (12)	72
Jennifer Grewar (13)	73
Aisling Goodey (12)	73
Tom Phillips (14)	74
Scott Ralston (12)	74
Alex Dolan (13)	75
Jenni Hagan (13)	75
Christine Reid (14)	76
Mark Pringle (13)	76
Suzy Boath (12)	77
Stewart Darling (13)	77
Alistair Brown (13)	78
Jonathan Irons (12)	78
Maud Sampson (13)	79

Hunter High School, East Kilbride

Jenna Ballantyne (12)	79
Cassie Rossiter (12)	80

Invicta Grammar School, Maidstone

Alice Gillham (15)	81
Emma Rippon (12)	81
Rachel Foreman (12)	82
Becky Holden (12)	82
Jessica Lomas (12)	83
Poppy Tester (12)	84
Emily Williams (11)	85
Jasmine Jakubuwski (12)	86
Jessica White (12)	87

LACE Service, Halifax

Katie Brown (14)	88

Lady Margaret School, London
Charlotte Coekin (12)	89
Laura Turner (12)	90
Beatrix Lovell-Viggers (12)	91
Julia Huettner (12)	92

Lymm High School, Lymm
Marleena Cronvall (13)	92

Mid Yell Junior High School, Shetland
Natasha Ogilvie (13)	93
Tanya Marie Finnie (13)	93
JJ Smiles (13)	94
Merryn Jane Tonner (13)	94
Zandra Williamson (13)	95
Kerry Reanne Nicholson (13)	95
Stephanie Caroline Keith (12)	96
Jack Jamieson (13)	96
Sophie Lamb (13)	96

Northease Manor School, Rodmell
Emma Coleman (13)	97

Onslow St Audrey's School, Hatfield
Anna Willis (12)	97
Stephanie Masvodza (11)	98

Perth High School, Perth
Micha Jayne Thompson (12)	98
Lachlan Gillies (12)	99
Kayleigh Maud (13)	100
Iain Ness (13)	100
Matt Burbridge (13)	101
Kirsty Hazelton (13)	101
Christopher Ewing (12)	102
Katie Malloy (12)	102
Rhona Donaldson (13)	103
Camrie Hole (13)	103
Ross Hunter (13)	104

Seán Kennedy (13)	104
Casey Martin	104
Rosie Christie (13)	105
Amber Martin (12)	105
Nicole Bright (13)	106
Anna Taylor (12)	106
Mark Mitchell (13)	107
Rebecca McCann (12)	108

Royal High School, Bath
Sian Denning (11)	108

St Gerard's School Trust, Bangor
Jessica Watters (11)	109
Benjamin Hughes (11)	110
Jack William Stanmore (11)	110
Alex Brown (11)	111

St Ives School, St Ives
Stacey Jane Palmer (12)	111

St Joseph's Academy, London
Peter Marezana (16)	112

South Wirral High School, Wirral
Jessica Elliott (12)	113
Tanya Citrine (13)	113
Daniel Tyler (14)	114
Danny Ashworth (11)	115
Lucy Vaughan (11)	116
Sam Jones (11)	117
Richard Davies (12)	117
John Jones (11)	118
Holly Chrishop (12)	118
Amy Louise Down (14)	119
Liam Forrest (12)	119
Matthew Drew (12)	120
Joel McCann (12)	120
Imogen Merrick (12)	121
Gemma Murray (11)	121

Emma Bonett (11)	122
Mathew Purcell-Jones (12)	122
Ben Davies (13)	123
Becky Green (12)	123
Heather Jones (15)	124
Amy Goddard (12)	124
Rebecca Cross (12)	125
Sophie Hughes (14)	125
Charlotte Murray (13)	126
Carol Colquhoun (12)	126
James Shell (12)	127
Joshua Phillips (13)	127
Heather Rankin (11)	128
Kate Patterson (13)	128
Lisa Moore (12)	129
Sophie Dawson (13)	130
Hannah Davies (13)	130
Georgina Treadwell (13)	131
Sai Howes (13)	131
Lauren Clyne (15)	132
Sarah Holden (13)	132
Sarah Jones (12)	133
Peter Shell (11)	133
Stuart Mackenzie (14)	134
Sam Busby (13)	134
Alexandra Ellen Moss (11)	135
Andrew Thompson (12)	135
Rebecca Edwards (11)	136
Jack Ithell (12)	136
Michael Williams (11)	137
Robyn Eccleston (11)	137
Sam Stewart (11)	138
Yvonne Stewart (12)	138
Jack Powell (13)	139
Kerry Ly (13)	139
Zoe Russell-Baugh (11)	140
Lee Russell (11)	140
Scott Gibson (12)	141
Sam Chan (11)	141
Stacey Moran (13)	142
Zoe Kilpatrick (12)	142
Daniel John Owen (12)	143

Michael Higgins (11)   144
Deborah Liu (14)   145

The College High School, Erdington
Kelly McEntee (14)   146

The Community School of Auchterarder, Auchterarder
Hayley Kitch (12)   147
Christina Davidson (11)   148
Matthew Anderson (12)   148
Claire Sneddon (11)   149
Sarah Langlands (12)   149
Ailsa Dann (12)   150
Anne McPhillimy (12)   151
Daniel Ghamgosar (13)   152
Zack Fummey (11)   152
Greg McArthur (11)   153
Kris Grimes (12)   153
Ben Warrington (12)   154
Patricia Mennie (13)   155
Martin Slamon (11)   156
Marc Hill (11)   156
Mairi Urquhart (12)   157
Ryan Miller (12)   157
Roslyn Andrews (13)   158
Charlie McArthur (13)   159
Thomas MacLaren (13)   160
Sam Mailer (13)   161
Jaqueline Hayburn (13)   162
Jenny Hutton (13)   163
Gemma Hughan (13)   164
Nicola Ross (13)   165

The Compton School, London
Natalie Richardson (14)   166
Benjamin Tinslay (13)   167
Edward Reade Banham (15)   168
Karl Jackson   169
Olivia Katis (13)   170
Adam Nikpour (12)   171

Nicholas Nicolaou (12)	172
Halima Mohammed (14)	173
Jo Taylor (14)	174
Gemini Tailor (14)	175
Tejas Depala (15)	176
Jessica Sofizade (12)	177
Kayan Poon (14)	178
Carole Walsh	179

Wansdyke Special School, Bath
Calvin Ellis (15)	180

Websters High School, Kirriemuir
Arran Middleton (17)	181
Emma Craddock (14)	182

Wilson Stuart Special School, Erdington
Alex Hackett (14)	183
Linh Hoang (15)	183
Adrian Holloway, Kenetia Thompson & Joe Spence (14)	184
Katy Evans (14)	184
Callum Mucklow & Laura Tomlinson (14)	185
Gurdeep Kainth (13)	185
Zubair Rehman (14)	186
Toni Bird (14)	186
Victoria Bates (15)	187
Nathan Green (14)	187
Dominique Levy (16)	188
Mithun Soul (13)	188
Jade Hinsley (12)	189
Kirsty Turner (13)	189
Saad Ashraf (14)	190
Jason Micklewright (15)	190

The Poems

Silence

They say silence is bliss,
A gift if you will,
All your problems can melt away,
If you're quietly thinking and still.

Silence is like meditation,
Getting in touch with your mind,
Silence brings answers and realisations,
That you may not easily find.

Silence is the best option,
In your thoughts it lurks,
After all the truth is,
In silence is the way God works.

Here is another side to silence though,
It can slow down the way time goes by,
Sometimes silence can be unbearably lonely,
So lonely you want to cry.

Silence is not always easy,
Some people don't like it at all,
And the eerie feeling it can bring,
Can drive you up the wall.

Silence can bring depression,
Silence can bring tears,
Silence can be calming,
Music to your ears.

Some people hate it,
Some people cherish it,
Some people fear it,
Some people dread it.

Siani Rahman (13)

Don't Let Me Die Mummy

A school bus set down the roadway
With a teacher and a mum,
To the Lake District they were heading,
Everyone should have come.

A stupid teacher jumped right in,
Said it was fine, OK.
Called a boy who was next in line,
Who thought it was OK.

A boy called Max followed the teacher,
The water was a killer,
Max jumped right in the water,
Colder than a chiller.

Max suddenly started to struggle,
The teacher tried to help,
Max became weak and feeble
The teacher couldn't help.

Max's mum, Trish, jumped right in,
The boy didn't want to die,
Trish became unconscious,
His mum didn't want to cry.

Max started to drift away from his mum,
A boy of 13 jumped to save Trish,
Max's mum suddenly came around
The teacher was no sir!

Max's body was found downstream
Teacher thought he was clear
Trish was very heartbroken,
Teacher in jail for a year.

Danni Walpole (12)

Monlife

Television blaring its square message,
Eyes drinking in every mindless detail,
Embroidered sofa, the seat of no state,
Time passes, but in the Home nothing changes,
Stale air lies like a lazy mist on the moor,
Dust blankets all in its stifling embrace,
While I, I sit and stare, stare and sit,
Endless monotony, the thoughtless territory,
Waiting in vain for some stop, some Change.

Computer glaring, errored obscenity,
Boredom settles and mind wanders to lust,
Hand slips under mass-produced pine table,
Time passes, but in the Office nothing changes,
Eyes search, suspicion written all around,
Great sigh of content. Glance back to same screen,
Great sigh of depression, fidget phase starts,
Stationery drawn up, war of the pens,
Waiting in vain for some stop, some Change.

Whiteboard shining, reflected fluorescence,
Unfathomable, infallible data sets,
Head propped up by palm, eyes simmer downward,
Time passes, but in the School nothing changes,
The endless drone drowns any sentient thought,
Rumbles of impatience whilst time ticks by,
Slipping through my vulnerable fingers,
Each moment precious, each moment gone, yet still
Waiting in vain for some stop, some Change.

Samuel Landau (15)

As The Blood Does Pour

If I stayed longer
Would you love me more?
Give you time to ponder
I know I'm just that chore
I'm just that thought
In the back of your mind
December, December rain
You stopped being kind
No cry, no gain
November, November rain
As the blood does pour
I will run
I will score
Forever against the clock
Tick-tock, tick-tock
Black and white
Red and blue
Love at its height
Because of you
I will run
Face so cold
Hands so blue
Thinking, thinking of you
No cry, no gain
July, July rain
Holding, holding you
January, January rain.

Chantal Skett (13)

Snow

A perfect sheet of glistening, powdery snow.
It looks so perfect,
But you are haunted with the knowledge that if you were under it
You would be *dead!*

It looks so perfectly white,
Lying on the ground,
But it can be made brown and yellow
With the mud on your shoes.
You know that if you walk across it,
You would ruin it,
Forever.

Like feathers falling from a tiny angel's wing,
It flutters to the ground like a spiderweb,
That has been torn to the floor,
As it whirls weightlessly,
To become one with the snow,
Where it will remain on the ground
Until spring.

Aoibhinn Byrom (11)

My First Day At School

There goes the bell - *ring, ring, ring,*
It's time for school,
Big school where the big kids dunk your head,
Where big kids swat our tie,
Where big kids . . . ooh I don't want to go.

I'm going in, it's huge,
There's all the big kids staring, laughing.
Oh look, there's Steph and Becks,
Hello! Hello! We get to the classroom.
My teacher's massive, a gentle giant,
He's OK and the older kids, they aren't that bad,
In fact, I quite enjoyed it.

Sasha Cox

Why Do I Remember?

It's funny I remember,
I wonder why I see
Mum placing the angel on the Christmas tree
My dog Pisha licking at her fur
Dad giving the coffee, one third and final stir.
The scent of snowballs
The cutlery so clean
It's funny I remember,
I wonder why I see

So odd that I remember,
I wonder why I see
Hair blowing backwards running a cross-country,
A pair of old socks, thick with mud to toe
With teachers - home in a soft top (embarrassing as you know)
The taste of my sweat
All so proud of me
So odd that I remember,
I wonder why I see

Always seem to remember,
I wonder why I see
The man named Willy Wonka shouting at me
Dreams of him through the nights
Nightmares haunt, the man of fright
Only a child
A horror to me
Always seem to remember
I wonder why I see

It's weird that I remember,
I wonder why I see
The woman from the blind charity looking at me
A blue McLaren in a magazine,
Mum always voting for 'Conservative Party'
The sound of raindrops
A Spanish friend and me
It's weird what I remember
I wonder why I see

Silly things I remember,
I wonder why I see
The day at 'Jail House Rock' with Elvis Presley
Scrumptious food - a great party
Dancing shouting - fun and glee
Music and screams
My friends and me
Silly things I remember
I wonder why I see

Why do I remember?
I wonder why I see
All the things that I remember which seem to calm me
Cries and screams, wishes and dreams
In my mind, it's not what it seems
All my thoughts
A lifetime of *me*
Why do I remember?
I wonder why I see.

Cheri Allcock (14)

Cheetah

As I crawl
Silently
Through the forest
A branch
Snaps.
I jump.
I sprint
After the animal.
It is fat and
Juicy.
I pounce
As fast as a bullet.
It's mine!

Leah Ormerod (12)

Fear Is . . .

Fear is a dark, stormy night,
Spiders running in your bed,
Ghosts humming over your head.
Fear is owls twitching,
Late at night
Witches and zombies make it a fearful sight.
Fear is a graveyard at night
No lights, just bats and vipers
Fear is the hiss of a snake,
A screech of a bat,
And a whistle of the dead
Fear is walking up to the graveyard
Seeing a ghost,
Hearing the humming over only one small, dark grave
Goosebumps pop up on my arms
Just one stream of sweat runs down my face.

Never get closer,
                Beware!

Maxine Churcher (12)

The Girl

The snow fell like feathers in the wind,
landing on her soft blonde hair,
seeming as if she'd never sinned,
with a life full of care,
she cared for her mother,
she cared for her dad,
she cared for her brother,
she also cared for her lad,
the snow started falling harder and harder,
creating a soft white sheet,
her boyfriend was putting his thoughts in order,
she was thinking of a place to meet.

Christopher Newman (16)

Dazzer, Cazzer And Shazzer

I know a boy called Darren
His girlfriend, she's called Sharon
They work twenty-four-seven
They deserve to live in Heaven
He was going to be a dad
That made him mad
She wanted to be a mother
And she wanted nothing other
So she wanted him to leave
And he went to live with Steve
He met a girl called Karen
And she fell in love with Darren
So they set a wedding date
They weren't going to be late
So now he's finished with Sharon
And now he's married to Karen
The ring was so big
Just like her wig
Will they live happily ever after
In joy and in laughter?

Nathan Smith (12)

Hallowe'en

H appy I am for getting sweets.
A ll the people trick or treat.
L ovely fireworks sparkle in the sky.
L ittle spiders crawl along as they dance with the song.
O ld witches ride along with a broomstick and a song.
W e dress up with our masks and cloaks.
E vil people don't give us sweets.
E veryone is happy that the witches have gone.
N ow our Hallowe'en party can carry on.

Kerry McDaid

The Twin Towers

It was a normal New York day,
The Trade Center towers standing tall,
But in a few moments,
They were about to fall.

The staff in the building,
Didn't realise danger was near,
Because on its way was a devil bird,
And an explosion they were about to hear.

The plane took aim,
The target was found.
Smash! The rubble and debris fell,
The plane's ruins fell to the ground.

The public ran as fast as they could,
Dodging the debris that fell.
The rescue team fought their way in,
The trapped people going through Hell!

The terrible day wasn't over,
To come was more pain,
Because on its way nearby,
Was another hijacked plane.

Ricky Leftly (13)

The Ice Cream Van

It was 35 degrees,
And there wasn't even a breeze,
Some people went to the swimming pool,
But soon it got full,
And even when they put the fan on high,
It wouldn't stop the heat from passing by,
So when the ice cream van went past,
People ran very fast,
Because they knew it would make them very cool,
Cooler than the fan and cooler than the swimming pool.

Salih Abdoun Mohammed (11)

The Day Of Respect - The Day Of Silence Remembrance Day

It's raining, it's pouring,
Dead bodies on the ground.

It's raining, it's pouring,
Without bombs flying through the air, there is no sound.

It's raining, it's pouring,
Close relatives' and friends' bodies have been found.

It's foggy and cold now,
Winston Churchill speaks aloud.

It's foggy and cold now,
Remember whom you have lost and always be proud.

It's foggy and cold now,
There is silence in the streets today.

It's foggy and cold now,
This is the one day we sit in silence for today is Remembrance Day.

Rachel Kennedy (15)

Mi Grandparents Come From Jamaica

Mi grandparents come from Jamaica,
the land they call their home,
they miss their family and friends,
and dem sweet mango trees.

Now mi grandparents live in Birmingham
but them miss Jamaica so
Dem say Jamaica is better than Birmingham
but I don't know.

I don't know what Jamaica is like
but all I know is my grandparents,
dem luv it.

Chanelle Bryan (12)

Hell

It's dark down there,
Underneath everything,
The soil, sand and water,
There lies the Devil, the king.

He's nasty, he's vile,
He'll punish you, he'll beat you,
He'll change your life completely,
You'll be horrified.

You'll be put to slavery,
And be frightened to death,
You'll wish you'd been good,
And treated others the same.

So be your best,
It's up to you,
Go to Heaven or
Go to Hell!

Minakshi Neelam Samrai (14)

Winter's Sleepers

Winter's whisper crying,
through prying opened eyes,
I see before my face a peace which thou despise.
Thou is not serenity to one's own depth unearth,
the thing I see before me I clasp its last words.
When winter is no longer, when spring is left to bear,
when its inclemency is not now here, nor is what was there.
It does not live any longer,
It does not breathe anymore,
It is not now sentient, it died and left its spoor.
Its scent leaves a memory,
of the creature which once was there,
that died in the coldness of winter
no one to remember or care.

Belinda Forde (13)

Counting And Wasting

Dreaming into oblivion.
Possibilities spread before me,
My opportunities are open,
I can choose my own future,
My path through the maze of life,
My way.

The blessing of individuality,
In the bliss of some's ignorance.
Passed-up chances,
Left.
Forgotten.
A waste of so many chances.

Space and soul,
The values slowly lower together.
Thrown-away choices and chances,
Ruined and pointless,
Worthless.
And a new day begins.

Jacqueline van Zetten (15)

My Sister Jessica

My sister Jessica is a . . .

Control-keeper
Chocolate-eater
Sleep-talker
Boy-lover
Room-wrecker
Dress-designer
School-skipper
Language-learner.

Sophie Falco (12)

What Is An Angel?

So
What *is* an angel?
What does it mean?
Do you wake and see something,
Or is it a dream?

Do they prowl around your bedstead in the middle of the night
In a shimmer of magic, a pure golden light?
Do they walk by your side as if holding your hand?
Can they make you see clearly their own fantasyland?

Or

Do they simply exist in the eyes of the holy
And attend to the old, the dying, the young or the poorly?

Or

Do they simply exist in stories and
Books
Christmas cards
Craft shops
Markets
Garden centres
Galleries
Department stores
Supermarkets
And cheap, tacky places where tourists will look?
Are they golden and glittery
Hard or soft?
Do you find them in Harrods or your old granny's loft?
Are they plastic or paper
Or real flesh, blood and bone?
Do they sing like a choir,
Or speak in dull monochrome?

So
What is an angel?
Tell me,
What *should* I see?
I *need* to reason,
I *want* to believe,
I feel that *my* angel
Is a billowing cloud of iridescent splendour
Bright, colourful, glittering and proud,
A being to protect *me*, to shelter and calm.
To guide, love me and *keep me from harm*
To share in my laughter and run through the stars
With my dreams in her hands
And my hopes in her arms.

Lorna-Marie Gilyeat (14)

Aunt Jane's Birthday Poem

Today is Jane's birthday, everyone is having fun,
But the party has not yet begun!
Today is Jane's birthday, the weather is bad.
Even my dad does not like it!
The sun goes in, the clouds are high,
We have to keep saying, 'Goodbye' to the sun,
'Hello' to the rain.
Then it does it all again,

But it is still *Jane's* birthday!

Erin Maloney-Cox (8)

Love Is Blind

You're miles away
And every day I pray
That you'll be back someday
Oh come what may

Why does everything keep rewinding?
Can't it just be everlasting?
I miss you so much
If only we could touch

I close my eyes and I see you
I know my love for you was true
But now it's a different case
Because I can't seem to find a trace

You're the only one who can heal my heart
The speed at which I've fallen apart
The crystal sea I gaze upon
Brings back memories that still live on

Your soul is with me everywhere I go
Chances of me being with you are low
I laid down everything for you
Didn't you see my love was true?

You're all I ever need
And still I continue to plead
I need the warmth that you provide
And I'll never let it slip or slide

When you're in my arms
I see your lovely charms
The time it hit the base
You were a loss I could not replace!

When I reach out my hand
I finally understand
That I can't turn the hands of time
And bring back what once was mine

I don't know why I couldn't see
When it was right there in front of me
I don't know what I tried to find
Now I know what is meant by 'Love is blind'!

Jenny Wong (16)

Inside My Head

There's a lightning storm
inside my head,
where crows start peeping,
where ash-filling skies
are keeping near,
animals run,
onto the pier.
There goes a cat.

There's a lightning storm
inside my head,
where tumbling trees
crack and break in two,
the strikes are tall,
very loud bangs.
I think it's cool.
There goes a cat.

There's a lightning storm
inside my head,
beside a driveway
a car sets alight,
what a big fright,
it is raining
of course at night,
in the month of May.

Jonathan Cox (11)

It's Not Fair

It's not fair, life's not fair,
It's not fair when you want someone to be there
when they can't, it's not fair,
It's not fair when you can't bring life back into death,
It's not fair when someone else takes someone's place,
It's not fair when everyone is getting along, why should you?
It's not fair, why should you be blamed for someone else's mistakes?
It not fair when you want to be there with them but you can't,
It's not fair when you've lost something you can't find,
It's not fair when someone comes along and wrecks everything,
It's not fair when you want to see someone and you can't,
It's not fair when you want to be with someone but you can't,
It's not fair when you say, 'Merry Christmas' and they can't say
                                                                       it back,
It's not fair when death overcomes everyone and anyone,
Death isn't fair!

Natalie Gibson (14)

Santa's Coming

Santa's coming, run and hide,
Jump and hop and skip and glide,
Don't pretend to be asleep,
He can see in your mind deep,
You can't fool the man in red,
Hurry up and get to bed!
Pull those covers up high,
You have been good, don't you sigh,
You'll get presents, big and small,
Whether you are small or tall,
Don't forget to thank your mam and dad,
For all those times you made them mad,
Santa's coming, run and hide,
Jump and hop and skip and glide.

Stacey Roberts (12)

My Computer

My computer has files and files,
So many I put them in piles.
The memory gets bigger and bigger,
I have to dig deeper and deeper
Down and down I go

I finally find the long-lost file
In the deepest and deepest, longest pile,
It has pages and pages
If I print it, that's all my wages
Down and down I go

Time's nearly up, time's nearly up,
My sister says, 'Hurry up.'
I say, 'Why? You are only a kid!'
Then she says, 'Go away,' and then called me a squid!
Down and down I go.

I call her a name
She says it is very lame,
I go down
With a frown!

Rishi Patel (13)

Untitled

The princess lies within her chambers,
Never does she leave the room.
Betrothed to the one she does not love,
She weeps for a forbidden groom.

The groom lies within the prison,
For every day he has cried.
The tears running down his shameful face,
He's mourning for his bride.

Kiran Perry & James Quirke (13)

Fear

The overwhelming desire to love you has overtaken
And now I fear you, fear losing you.
Fear loving you, only to get shot down.
My longing to be near you stops me moving closer.
I fear you'll pull away. Fear you won't want me.
Fear you'll turn from me if I get too close.
A growing happiness stops me smiling.
I fear you'll hurt me. Fear you'll upset me.
Fear you'll disappear, leave me.
My trust in you grows, making me bottle things up
For fear of it not working. Fear that you don't trust me.
Fear you're hiding things from me.
The need to kiss you makes me hesitate. Think.
I fear you don't want me to. Fear you'll push me away.
Fear you'll walk away if my lips touch yours.
Fears I have don't go away.
They grow each time you're away.
I sit. Think too much. I get worried, paranoid.
I fear you're thinking of ways to let me down.
Thinking of ways to end what we have.
I fear you only because of what you are able to do.
Something I cannot stop, something only you can decide.
Something I wouldn't dream of doing to you.
I try to love you but I fear you won't love me back.

Kaz Davies (16)

Life

Sometimes life's good,
Sometimes life's bad,
A good time is when you can comfort someone,
A bad time is when you cut yourself accidentally.
One thing, however, gets me through it all
Friends and family.

Terri Masters (14)

Baby Blue

'A cot fit for a prince,' they said
As they adorned his little bed.
Knitted quilt from aunt abroad
Hours spent for the unborn adored.
Pillows of finest eiderdown
Painted circus, waving clown
Softest doe-eyed rabbit toy
All this for their baby boy.

Empty that room forever lies
Silent, no baby laughs or cries
No attempt to clear the mocking things
To her dead son the mother sings.
No child shall ever run their home
Run and jump, leap or roam,
A baby wished for, much-loved son
They watch the cot where there is none.

Lucy Laycock (15)

The World

The world is filled with love
The world is filled with hate
The world is filled with millions of people and just a
                                        few can be our mates
The world is filled with lies
The world is filled with spies
The world is filled with silent cries

It's our world so we should treat it with care
An alien would probably say, 'I wouldn't want to live there!'
Let's pick up the litter
And make it better for the future
It's only one life we have, one life in this place
So I don't know about you, but I don't want it to go to waste.

Sarah-Bayeya Nyemba (13)

Release

The water enveloped me,
All around my skin,
I felt the cold wrap round me,
Now I don't know whether to sink or swim.

I tried to tell you of my pain,
But you just laughed and that's why I'm here,
Because I took the brunt of your evil,
Every ridicule and every leer.

Why did you never listen?
The world doesn't revolve around you,
You watched everything I did,
Followed my every move,
Well now I can't let you invade me,
I won't allow you to take over,
With your poisonous touch,
Because you will not dictate what I will do.

There are days that I love you,
And days I do hate your very soul
There are days I need to unleash,
To wipe out all that is sin and dull,
But I have a saviour,
When the fury does end,
You will experience my love and rage,
When the fury doth end,
And I will be free from my cage!

Sam Mustafa (14)

River

Rabbit and deer
So very near
My icy fingers touch
Then slide away
For not today
I will see them much
As they run and fly
I flow and tumble
Over stone and earth
They call and cry
I giggle and bubble
With contagious mirth
Keep far from yon slender pine
Roots firm in ground of peat
The forest wind
Will sweep you clear
Off your nimble feet
Come any day to a forest glade
To watch me passing close
See me reach my destination
The free, enchanting coast
The salty air, I can almost smell it
Holds me like a spell
Watch me as I
Say goodbye
To this lonely forest dell.

Jenny Clark (11)

Natural Sad Way

The swirling size,
It swallows the skies.
Wind and gravity crossed.

Those poor ripened trees,
Are robbed of their leaves,
But all in a natural sad way.

The plants bend back,
Their spines will snap.
Transformation done no cost.

The clouds have sinned,
The cruelty of wind,
As the plants bend over and sway.

The strongest roots,
And the weakest of shoots,
Join as the surface gets tossed.

The twist gets tired,
Its bottom still spired,
Now dilutes the blue sea dark grey.

But after the grind,
Not a human would mind,
Because nothing of theirs is lost.

Tom Webb (13)

The Kiss

As our lips touched, I knew it felt right,
That sensational feeling I had on that night.
His mouth was so soft, it made my legs tingle,
Oh how glad I am that I am not single.
My stomach was filled with fluttering butterflies,
But it was OK when we said our goodbyes.
From this day forth, I'm filled with bliss,
All because of that fantastic kiss.

Amy Hawkins (13)

Be Mine

All I want is you but what am I to do?
Just wait till I turn bitter and blue?
All I want is you and I know you want me too.

I dream about you every night.
My heart feels warm when you are in my sight.
In my daydreams I picture your face.

My love for you came at such a pace.
It was as if my heart had been set on a race.
A race I wanted to win but if I did it would be a sin.

A sin for you have a girl in your life,
A girl who would love to be your wife.

Though I know he will never be mine
I suppose to have my dreams is fine.
But his smile will always shine
And I will always wish he were mine . . .

Emma Tarbuck (16)

Where Have You Gone?

You have gone! I don't know where
Mum says you're in the sky somewhere.

Are you in a hot air balloon?
Will you becoming back soon?

I'm looking after Jasper your dog
He sits up high on the log.

I thought I was going with you
Mum said, 'No!'
I cried, 'Boo-hoo!'

Why are you in the sky
Flying up high, so high?

Mum said you had passed away
What does that mean? Mum won't say!

Lauren Davidson (12)

A Pen

Meandering lazily over perfect postcards,
Lolling in pencil pots and glinting jam jars.
Sliding smoothly through a magician's ear,
Labouring across love letters, licking the paper.
Snaking down streets - forming a map,
Looping boxes for Lady Luck.
Tickling walls as it plays with crime,
Swivelling slowly in lukewarm mouths.
Swimming in briefcases, nestled in pockets,
Hurtling 'Happy Birthday' onto gleaming cards.
Gliding guiltily over cream coloured cheques,
Tucked into pencil cases - an uncomfortable bed.

The days drain out, the replicas roll in,
As it rocks beneath in a sluggish sleep.
Grazing the paper, scratching the sheets,
Trailing its failing fading blood.
Shaken with rage, jabbing at corners,
To find a pattern of dents in the page.
Lidless, emptied, gnawed to the tip,
Losing its grip as its grip loses it.

Xanthe Batt (15)

Mum

Mum you are number one,
'Cause when I was small you used to wipe my bum.

Mum, you are funny,
You're always giving me money.

Mum, you don't get really mad,
You are nothing like my dad.

Mum, you always buy me presents at special times,
And always buy and read the 'Evening Times'.

Kirsty Wood (14)

You

I wish for the day
When we could be together,
I wish you could stay,
Here forever and ever.
I wish you were here,
I long for your touch,
For your voice in my ear,
I want to hold you so much.

I hope for the day,
When you're here through the night,
When I have my way,
Everything wrong would be right.
I hope for your eyes,
That would at last be,
Staring deep into mine,
You're the only one I want to see.

I dream of the day,
When you would put your hand
Into mine, there to stay,
That's all I need to understand,
I dream that some day
We'll be together once more,
But the more I think, the more I say,
I miss you so much more.

Rebecca Wade (13)

Hate

I hate you so much I could scream
So loud that I would burst my bloodstream
You're such a waste of time and space
That I want you to leave my place
I feel claustrophobic with the way you nag me
The way you scream and yell at me.
How you push me down with your deceitful ways
I will put an end to my suffering days.

I don't love or need you anymore.
My black eyes or the clothes you tore.
Thinking you had it all your way
But I'm going to make you leave today
You can take your fake memories of us
I'll get back on my feet, I will sus
I'll mend my torn aching heart
And my broken bones - every part

It's too late for you now
You tried to get rid of me but how?
Kill me off by beating me to death
I'd tell you how much I hate you 'til my last breath
You can keep on playing your game
But I swear you'll never be the same
Not with your faulted and twisted soul
I'd rip off your head and stick it on a pole!

Laura James (16)

He Sits Alone

He sits alone
On the park bench helplessly staring
Though he cannot see
He can still hear
He can hear the birds singing in the morning sky
He can hear ducks happily talking to each other
While children laugh and play spreading crumbs for the ducks
He knows when people walk past
As he can hear the gravel crumble under their feet
He sits alone
On the park bench helplessly staring
Though he cannot see
He can still smell
He can smell the freshly cut grass lying in the sun
He can smell the flowers of spring blooming in the gentle breeze
He can smell the glory of the nearby burger bar
Sizzling in the hot weather
He sits alone
On the park bench helplessly staring
Though he cannot see
He can still feel
He can feel the cool breeze making him feel cold
He can still feel the warm, soft fur
Of his guide dog
Waiting to take him home.

Claire Komar (11)

The Fox Vs Man

The fox,
Only beasts they are,
But do not be fooled,
The fox is cunning,
So comes by night,
When it shall strike.

The fox,
Their lands near and far,
Under the tree you are cooled,
The fox prepares
For your nightmares,
But shall wait for night,

The fox,
But I am not fooled,
The fox is clever,
But more than me? Never!
I set a trap,
And take a nap.

The fox,
It creeps out of its den,
Towards the rabbit pen,
Then all of a sudden,
Snap!
My trap is sprung.

Now who was fooled? Not me but *you!*

Ray Barron (12)
Aberdour School, Tadworth

Summer

Yellow:
Soft chrome sand
Bright honey sunflowers bowing their heads
Pale lemon sunrises

Orange:
Bright searing midday sun
Glaring down on velvet wallflowers

Red:
Poppies bringing back sad memories
Sweet smells of crimson roses
Juicy strawberries and magenta-streaked sunsets

Blue:
Clear sapphire morning skies
Spiky cornflowers
Glittering turquoise seas

Green:
Peridot leaves in a summer breeze
Lush iridescent grass underfoot
Malachite weeds strangling everything
Emerald creepers snaking up walls

Indigo:
Storm clouds bursting open
Fat drops of summer rain
Long mauve shadows in the evening
Falling on quiet lawns

Violet:
Scented lavender, ripe plums
Gentian sunsets fading into the warm summer nights

These are the summer colours in my head.

Andrew Phillips (12)
Aberdour School, Tadworth

The Fox

There was I, on the ground,
When all at once I heard a sound.
A shake, a snap, a cry, a crunch,
Sounded like the 'thing' had found its lunch.

Then I saw it standing there,
Only a fur coat did it wear,
Its crimson nose was stained with blood,
Its scarlet paws, tarnished with mud.

Two pointy ears stuck from the head,
The body was a shocking red.
His underbelly, soft and white,
It seemed to glow within the night.

Once it finished all its fun,
Back to its den, see it run.

Alexander Gibbons (12)
Aberdour School, Tadworth

Summer

Summer is a great time,
Full of sunshine and heat,
We can play outside,
Sometimes in bare feet!

Summer means long school holidays,
And fun days at the beach,
Picnics in the park,
Long evenings when it doesn't get dark.

Summer trees are full of leaves,
The flowers are full of scents,
Butterflies are colourful and bright
They are such a beautiful sight.

Joshua Chan-Lok (12)
Aberdour School, Tadworth

Moods
(Be anything!)

To make a promise,
To make a pact,
To make friendliness
An actual fact.

To do a drawing,
To do a painting,
To play music,
Entertaining.

To have trust,
To have knowledge,
The power of these
Is one's edge.

To smile,
To die,
To befriend,
To lie.

People can be anything they want,
For better or for worse is choice,
To lie and deceive others, for shame
Or to protect them from the truth.

Gordon Shephard (13)
Aberdour School, Tadworth

The Fox

There the fox watches for its prey,
Sitting there with a conniving plan,
Until he starts to creep around,
From night-time until day.

The time has come
Mr Rabbit comes out of his cage,
Mr Rabbit hops and hops,
But doesn't get away.

There Mr Rabbit is dying in pain,
But Mr Fox doesn't care,
He thinks about doing it all again.

Mr Fox is happy,
He's found his dinner,
So that must be the end of the day
Tomorrow he'll definitely do this all over again.

Mayuri Pattni (12)
Aberdour School, Tadworth

Dreams

I dreamed I was a racing car driver winning a race,
Normally I dream I am floating in space.
I dreamed I was a millionaire,
As well as a football player.
Or maybe a pilot in the Royal Air Force,
Maybe a jockey winning the Derby on my trusty horse.
A rock star who's got their own cool band,
Or an explorer who's discovered a completely new land.
An Olympic skier who's just won gold,
Or an Eskimo. That would be very cold!
There are loads of things I could be,
Actually, at the moment, I think I'll be me!

Daniel Pearson (12)
Aberdour School, Tadworth

Summer

Summer is a time of year
That we all enjoy
Summer is a time of year
When one girl meets one boy

Summer is a time of year
Almost everyone will love
Summer is a time of year
You're likely to spot a dove

Summer is a time of year
When animals come out
Summer is a time of year
When everyone just wants to shout

Summer is the time of year
When everyone should be friends

Summer is the time of year
The ultimate time for fun!

Sam Freeman (13)
Aberdour School, Tadworth

Special Day

Tom got out of his bed,
And pestered his mum about getting fed.

Food was the most important thing
To build strength for cross-country running.

The team would be chosen soon
The event would be this afternoon.

The master in charge, Mr Kirkham
Chose Tom but wasn't certain.

He ran the course just for fun
But was amazed when he won!

Stephen Hume (13)
Aberdour School, Tadworth

Moods

'Stop moaning Jonathan!'
'Did you do your homework?'
'I thought I told you to clean your football boots!'

If I was a fox, I could run about freely,
Without a care in the world.
I could sneak about,
And have a peek at the chicken run.

'Don't answer back Jonathan!'
'Speak up, I can't hear you!'
'Don't hunch your shoulders Jonathan!'
'Turn that television down!'

If I was an eagle I could fly up high,
Where nobody would go
And nobody would see me.
Feeling the wind against my feathers,
And putting all thoughts of parents out of mind.

Jonathan Matthews (13)
Aberdour School, Tadworth

Summer

In summer everything is just right,
The birds are in full flight,
And there is no bad weather,
Because everything is much better.
Everyone comes out in the sun,
All the way till the day is done,
And so everything is warm as it's becoming
But be prepared, winter is coming.

Christian Killoughery (12)
Aberdour School, Tadworth

The Fox

Mr Fox is very subtle
He always walks on all four paws
Unless he's a fox that's wily
Foxes are known as very good scavengers
As they will find their food or prey.

> Whether they're in the mood or not
> They will find food for their young
> As Mrs Fox will not be pleased
> If her other half does not provide
> The contents needed for her much loved family.

>> Sly Mr Fox knows where he is going
>> For his eyesight cannot be touched
>> In all good deeds he may do
>> Mr Fox will make sure that he'll make a kill
>> To show the world that he is the king of the garden.

Shahail Woodcock (12)
Aberdour School, Tadworth

Dreams

A mass of images roll around,
Full of strange facts and scenes.
You're present in the weirdest world,
The world of all your dreams.

You tumble into a blank, empty space,
Thrown into a place you don't know.
Your thoughts flicker by, one by one.
Your imagination is free to flow.

Colours zoom past at the speed of light,
And all reality has run away.
You lie there dreaming on and on
To find yourself awake the next day.

Emma Diggins (13)
Aberdour School, Tadworth

Pop Star

P retty as a princess singing on the stage
O nly she knows when she is off key
P eople watch her singing in melody

S inging on stage with no nerves
T eaching little children how to sing
A gile off stage but strong on stage
R eaching for her towel to say farewell.

Thomas Pearson (13)
Aberdour School, Tadworth

Beautiful Chaos

The harsh bay currents,
And the evil sight ahead,
Are swept away at sunset,
At the Golden Gate's bed.

The ever-changing weather,
And the dense fog . . . sometimes,
Make the evil sight hard to see,
From where the tourists dine.

The picturesque Angel Island,
And Alcatraz too,
Make tourists want to flock here,
For these things to do.

Involved in all this chaos,
Is a sight to see,
The bridge stands in all magnificence,
Intertwined within the scenery.

Kim Loughhead (15)
Alleynes High School, Stone

St Tropez

Ceaseless fine specimens of gaudy boats set the scene of the tranquil harbour,
Affluence lining St Tropez is seen dripping from satin coats
into the much-desired bay.
Purity resounds with white sails lifting high,
Market trade rises as tourists meander by.
Cobbled streets filled with mahogany tables peddle their unwanted belongings,
While the hustle and rush is heard from the perpetual thronging.
Impertinent merchants stand bellowing from stalls,
Challenging each other with increasingly louder calls.
Ocean views frame the idyllic scene,
With transparent waters lapping rocks pristine.
A combination of beauty and elegance surrounds this
bustling town of exclusive residence.

Roseanna Gray (15)
Alleynes High School, Stone

Friendship

Friendship is baby-blue
It tastes like hot Italian food
And smells like lavender
Friendship sounds like children's laughter.

Helena Oakes & Hannah Rickwood (12)
Babington House School, Chislehurst

War

War is the colour of a camouflaged suit,
And tastes like blood,
It smells like dead bodies,
War sounds like explosions killing innocent people,
And feels like loneliness.

Nicola Jarman (12)
Babington House School, Chislehurst

Bullying

Bullying is black
It tastes like sour lemons
It smells like sour milk
It looks like a hairy tarantula
It sounds like endless bombs
It feels like needles digging into your skin.

Lucie Bentley (12)
Babington House School, Chislehurst

Laughter

Laughter is bright green,
It tastes like fizzy cola bottles
And smells like fresh buds
Laughter looks like friends.
It feels happy.

Ha, ha, ha, ha.

Casey Adams
Babington House School, Chislehurst

Friendship

Friendship is multicoloured.
It tastes like candyfloss
And smells like a fairground.
Friendship looks like a rainbow.
It sounds like boys and girls splashing in puddles.
Friendship feels like a cuddly bear.

Holly Barker (12)
Babington House School, Chislehurst

Fear

Fear is black and brown
It tastes like dark chocolate
It smells like smoke
It looks like a blanket of black
It sounds like a nightmare
It feels like a cool chill.

Sûreya Ibrahim (12)
Babington House School, Chislehurst

Violence

Violence is red like blood trickling down a boy's body
When he has been viciously stabbed.
It tastes like a cold roast dinner.
It smells like dead and diseased rats.
It sounds like a baby's scream.
Violence is the hesitant steps of fear
That prevents you from moving forward.

Latisha Elliott (13)
Babington House School, Chislehurst

Happiness

Happiness is the colour of the sun
It tastes of sweet strawberries
Happiness is the smell of flowers in a field
It sounds of happy children playing
Happiness is joyful.

Sophie Walker (13)
Babington House School, Chislehurst

Violence

Violence is black,
It is like a vast nothingness,
It tastes like a mouldy banana,
And smells like cheesy feet,
Violence looks like a big foreboding wood,
The sound of violence is a never-ending scream,
It feels like the deadly venom of an angry snake
Viciously tearing into my skin.

Annabelle Tricks (12)
Babington House School, Chislehurst

Romance

Romance is a blushing red
It tastes like sweet strawberries
Romance smells like new-bloomed roses
It looks like a cuddly puppy
Romance sounds like a popping champagne bottle
It feels like a warm blanket.

Emma Griffin Beat (12)
Babington House School, Chislehurst

Starvation

Starvation is a murky-grey
And it tastes like nothing
It smells of dry flesh
It feels like the hot sun beating down on your back
It sounds like a screeching cat
Starvation is emptiness.

Lucy Colin
Babington House School, Chislehurst

It's A Free Country, Right?

Not when you have to beg for money,
In the damp and freezing cold,
When you lost your youth looking prematurely old.

Not when you have no bed,
Just a blanket in a shop door,
Lying in the darkness wishing you had more.

Not when you have friends
To go out with,
But the feelings of loneliness turn in to dead ends.

Now I don't think it's all a free country, right . . .

Danielle Aitken (14)
Brae High School, Shetland

The Things We Take For Granted

The things we take for granted are the things that they want most,
A parent to cuddle up to, or a nice warm piece of toast.

The things we take for granted are the things that they want most,
You eat proper meals, while they eat leftover roast.

The things we take for granted are the things that they want most,
You sleep in a nice warm bed,
When the most they get's a cardboard box.

The things we take for granted are the things that they want most,
Someone should really help them, but none will be the host!

Stewart Williamson (13)
Brae High School, Shetland

It's A Free Country, Right?

Not when you are filthy so you can't get a job.
Not when people bully you that's when you start to sob.

Not when you are so cold that you cannot feel your feet.
Not when the only music you hear are the buskers on the street.

Not when your place has been nicked because you went to the loo.
Not when the nights get so cold you wish to make it through.

Not when you can't change the channels because the TV is in the
                                                                                             shop window.
Now when the hostel is so full you have nowhere else to go.

Not when your stomach rumbles as the bin won't suffice your needs.
Not when no one wants to help you they won't do these deeds.

Not when your clothes do not fit you, you can't afford to buy more.
Not when you don't have an education, they talk to you like you're
                                                                                              a door.

Not when you get so upset you just want to die.
Not when you need a shower so bad people laugh as they go by.

Anya Charleson (14)
Brae High School, Shetland

It's A Free Country, Right?

I wake up in the morning happy, happy as can be.
I wake up in the morning wishing I could change me.
I dress myself in designer clothes to keep me from the cold.
I wear the same clothes, the ones that are battered and old.

I go and see my friends, the ones that are at my school.
I don't have any friends to see, they think I am too uncool.
I go home to eat my nice warm meal.
I can't afford to eat unless I make a deal.

I go and sit with my family to play a family game.
I go and sit in my doorway always just the same.
I make my way to my nice warm bed, time to rest my head.
I climb into my cardboard box wishing I was dead.

How can this be a free country
When you are homeless and growing old?
Wishing you were somewhere else
To keep you from the cold.

How can this be a free country when I am lying in my bed
And you are out on the streets nowhere to rest your head?

This is not a free country and I know why,
I have got the whole wide world and you just want to die.

Leanne Shedden (14)
Brae High School, Shetland

It's A Free Country, Right?

It's cold 'n' dark and I've got bruises on my leg,
But those rich little gits have warm, comfy beds.
They can go out, look good and have friends,
But when I wake up the same story starts, but feels like it never ends.

Now, imagine feeling like you've never showered,
Being beaten up and overpowered.

For free, they get proper meals in front of their heads,
But to get our meal, we have to do a deal instead.

When they get money, they can go out and buy clothes or a snazzy
cap,
But when we need money we have to beg or tap.

What I'm trying to say is . . .
I hate being smelly and never showered,
Always being overpowered,
Always hungry
And never having enough money.
I hate being homeless
And I hate being poor.
Sleeping on the pavement is always sore.
We've got to fight for a right,
But hey, the motto is, 'It's a free country, right?'

Thomas Wyeth (14)
Brae High School, Shetland

It's A Free Country, Right?

Not when you're hungry
And can't earn one pence.
Not when you're lonely
And nothing makes sense.

Not when you're begging
The people just shun you.
Not when you're pleading,
At least for a shoe.

Not when you're sleeping
Or trying at least.
Not when you're freezing,
Wanting a feast.

Not when you're tossing
Or when you're turning.
Not when you wake up,
Your body is burning.

Not when you want
A normal life again.
Not when you wish,
You had even a ten.

Not when you're looked down on,
No one gives a toss.
Not when you can't get a job,
They say, 'It's your loss.'

Not when your life's bad,
Nothing but a mess.
Not when you give up
And couldn't care less.

Siân Bryant (14)
Brae High School, Shetland

If Imagination Was Something . . .

It spills and gushes out of our minds,
Twisting and entangling everything around us.
It must be solid because it's always everywhere.
Yet, I know that when you touch it,
It blurs and smudges colour together.

The colours! All of them.
Even ones I've never seen before.
They swirl together like fog and mist.
I know it mustn't walk, it must float,
Like an immense, bursting cloud of colour,
Ready to rain sweet droplets below.

It tastes warm and sweet.
But if you were to swallow it,
It would send a cold, refreshing chill through you.
Mint, I think it tastes of sweet, fresh mint.
So strong, making you cry dewdrop tears.

Damp, freshly cut grass and morning dew is its smell.
Perhaps it is also a little fruity. Yes!
Fresh fruit! Apples! Damp apples!
Exactly what the word 'nectar' should smell like.

It is a cacophony of sound! Every sound!
Trumpets mostly, but soft interludes of a gentle harp.
Sometimes it is so loud the sound could burst eardrums.
But sometimes so soft, there must be silence to hear it.
Sometimes not even instruments, but gentle breathing
Because imagination is alive!

Suzy Pope (17)
Berwickshire High School, Duns

Hacker

In a dark room I am surrounded by computers.
Outside the sun is going down, as everyone else's day ends,
                                                mine begins.
I focus my mind on the task at hand.
On the cold glass, illuminated by the flickering light of my lamp,
                                          words flash and dance.
I wish I had a better life than this.
My computer beeps and hums in rhythm with my slow, steady
                                                    breathing.
My mum comes in and tells me to turn the light off
I have school tomorrow.

Richard Roberts (14)
Cardiff High School, Cyncoed

Pilot

Thirty thousand feet up in the sky I steer precisely.
Through the window, fluffy clouds surround me.
I think through my flight plan and every movement.
Three aeroplanes zoom past leaving long trails.
I wish I could speed up time to reach my destination.
I hear the heavy rumble of the engine
The air stewardess comes in ordering coffee.

Andrew Drayton (14)
Cardiff High School, Cyncoed

Life Of A Lawyer

In the courtroom, I sit next to my client.
Through the window I see the busy street life.
I think of how I will win the case.
I see the court rise for the judge.
I wish to be home, watching.
I hear the murmurs of the jury whispering.
My client approaches me anxiously.

James Abbott (14)
Cardiff High School, Cyncoed

Fog

Fog is like a black horse,
Dancing over the hills,
It twists and turns in a depressing way,
That's dark and evil and gloomy . . .

Swooping over the mountains,
Eating up the sun,
Suffocating the environment,
Cascading down the whispering roads,
Like a Formula 1 car . . .

It consumes whole villages at a time,
Like an evil beast,
Galloping through the howling valleys,
Groans and screams,
Like rumbling thunder through the sky.

Molly Shatwell (12)
Hayesfield School, Bath

The Midnight Cat

Late one night,
When everyone was asleep,
The midnight cat leapt out of his basket,
Outside he creeped.
Lurking through the dustbins,
Looking for something tasty.
Sticking its nose in smelly tins.
Suddenly the cat is seen by a filthy man,
The midnight cat runs, but the man catches up,
Can the midnight cat make it up the wall?
Yes he can.
The time has passed
The midnight cat is safe at last.

Lucy Sullivan (12)
Hayesfield School, Bath

Magical Cat

My mum while walking through the door
Spilt some magic on the floor,
Bits of this
And blobs of that
But most of it on my cat.

My cat turned magical straight away,
And in the garden went to play
Where she grew two massive wings
'Oh look,' cried Mum, pointing at the sky,
'I didn't know your cat could fly.'

Then with a swish of her tail,
She turned my mum into a snail.
So now my mum lives beneath a stone
And plods around a different home.

And I'm an ant and Dad's a mouse
And my cat's living in our house.

Hannah Woodland (11)
Hayesfield School, Bath

Hail

The hailstones cascade down from the furious clouds.
Punching down on the streets, drumming on the rooftops.
The icy blocks beat down and the sky turns an angry grey.
People outside wrestling with the monsters while trying to escape.
Gradually, the evil stones turn to little droplets,
Pattering onto the ground forming puddles.
The droplets then stop and the grey clouds float away
To reveal a glowing sun.

Esme Haughton (12)
Hayesfield School, Bath

Questions Of Life

Why not travel the world?
Why does school even exist?
Why eat off plates?
Why not eat buns in the mist?

Where can I eat a duck on a stick?
Where can I learn how to fly?
Where is the nearest balloon town?
Where is the sky in a pie?

Who discovered the Earth?
Who designed the moon?
Who's your favourite doctor?
Who ran away with the spoon?

What is googar in French?
What is a pig without a tail?
What are the meanings of life?
What is the use of a nail?

How do you know that a duck is a bird?
How do you know pigs can't fly?
How do you know a chick isn't a goose?
How do you know till you try?

Lizzie Thorn (11)
Hayesfield School, Bath

Rain

Rain is a thin blanket, a curtain of cold
A cascading capturer that locks you inside like a prison.
Sometimes it's just a repetitive, innocent pattering, a twirling gloom,
That will turn on you and smother you in a shivering cold.

Libby Skinner (12)
Hayesfield School, Bath

. . . What About You?

Simple things such as silvery raindrops
Are what I like the most.

Long, lazy lie-ins on Sundays;
A mother's inviting hug;
The rhythmic tick of a clock in a silent room; and dappled light.

The warm touch of summer sun on sand-covered skin;
Laughing till my tummy aches;
And dancing till my feet give in;
The moist earthy smell after a shower of rain;
The delicate flap of a bird's wings;
The snuffle of sleeping babies and puppies
And intertwining clouds in a picture-perfect sky.

The deep rumbling of thunder from all around;
The rustle of leaves in towering trees;
A flat stone skimming on a still lake
And warm breath hazily covering a starry sky on a clear night;
The smell of clean, crisp sheets
And dewy droplets enclosed in flower petals.
The more I think the more simple things I come to like.
What about you?

Roxanne O'Fee (14)
High School of Dundee, Dundee

Natural Beauty

Cascading water,
Reflecting pools,
Glistening and clear
That's what a waterfall should be.

Delicate petals,
Pristine leaves,
Gorgeous deep colours,
That's what a flower should be.

Green grassy glades,
Snow-capped peaks,
Fresh, clean air,
That's what a mountain should be.

Tall, blossoming trees,
Timid woodland animals,
All is still, but full of life,
That's what a forest should be.

A new surprise round every corner,
Everywhere wonders to be found,
Wherever you look is natural beauty,
That's what the world should be.

Rachael McLellan (12)
High School of Dundee, Dundee

People

Loud people laugh all the time
Love to be the centre of attention
Have not a care in the world
Are happy to be different
Happy to be noticed.

These people seem self-centred
They seem to be happy
But as a different person
I wonder what they'd think of the world.

Quiet people don't want to cause trouble,
Keep themselves to themselves.
They hate to be noticed
Though they might long to break free.

These people are hard to work out.
They are happy with who they are
But these people who hate to be noticed
Perhaps want to shine, but are scared to.

People like me, meaningful and deep
Try to understand everything.
We want to have a good time,
We want to fit in - not to stand out
People like me want to be understood.

Rachel Jones (13)
High School of Dundee, Dundee

What Makes Life Special?

I love . . .
Soft snow, crisp, no footprints,
brightly coloured, warming sunsets
and the black, star-filled sky which follows;
clear, woodland streams trickling down slimy rocks;
and the blossom trees full of buds.

I would miss . . .
Pink, fluffy cushions on a freshly made bed;
the feel of the cold side of the pillow;
a friendly smile welcoming and a cheeky grin!
Pink birthday cake, marshmallows, fluffy and white;
smooth rich chocolates.
All these I love.

What do I love?
Happy faces, loyal friends, people, family, strangers;
pattering droplets of rain falling from fluffy, white clouds;
a chilly wind, and the contrast of hot, sunny weather,
a burning-hot sun and below a beach, listening to the calming waves;
the sound of the sea . . . in a tropical seashell.

All these I love, but why?
They can't be bought by money,
They are precious things that would be dearly missed.

Rachel Coleman (13)
High School of Dundee, Dundee

Twelve O'Clock Twilight

At twelve o'clock twilight, the owls glide,
The ghostly horseman comes from his hide
The clumping hooves and rattling chain
He mounts his beast in the pouring rain.

The sounds of the horse hooves awakens the ghosts,
They come from their hollows, by this time you're toast.
Moaning and groaning and whispering and whining
Wailing and whimpering, they have just the right timing.
They swoosh over heads, hide under beds
Waiting for you to scream, argh!

The cackling witches are hearing this sound,
'Oh, let's get them, we'll show them they bound to come round.'
These ghostly creatures are out to find hunt
They'll find you and scare you, they never go blunt.
Mounted on brooms they cackle and shriek!
You'll hear them, I'm sure, their voices aren't weak!

These circling creatures, floating around
They'll lurk in the graveyards, that's their home ground.
You'll have to take care, watch out!
You might not be safe in your nice, cosy bed,
You'll have to try to scare them instead!

Vanita Nathwani (12)
High School of Dundee, Dundee

The Simple Things In Life

The things I love are the simple things in life.
They are of many shapes and sizes, sights and smells:
Warm bedclothes wrapped around me on a Sunday morning lie-in;
Lazy girl's nights in, slumped in front of a television with a bowl
of popcorn;
The indulgence of an ice cream on a scorching summer's day;
The tension of a ghost story being shared between friends.

Water cascading everywhere as I jump into the sea
To escape the tropical heat of my favourite holiday destination;
Fresh baking welcoming me home after a hard day's work on
a harsh, winter evening;
Lots of people playing music together in melodious harmony;
The merriment of a family gathered round a laden table for
Christmas dinner.

The smell of the pages of a brand new book;
The way a river twists and turns changing its course
Meandering slowly before diving head-first over a waterfall;
Spending quality time with friends and family, who stick together
through thick and thin.

These things are priceless and can never be replaced
Which makes them special to me.
I could not imagine my life without them.

Eilidh Firth (14)
High School of Dundee, Dundee

A Day On The Moon

We set off to the moon
Around about noon
In a rocket, covered in mould.

When we got there
The surface was bare
Just like we'd already been told.

But we smelled some cheese
In the moonly breeze
And got out crackers from where they'd been loaded.

Sometime later
We found Brie in a crater
And ate till we almost exploded.

On looking around
We found a great mound
Of deliciously creamy Edam.

There were rocks made of Cheddar
Gorgonzola and Cheshire
It was a cheesy Garden of Eden!

With the cheeses depleted
And our stomachs defeated
Our spaceship was leaving quite soon.

We had cheeses to sell
And stories to tell
Of our amazing day on the moon!

Josh Ivinson (12)
High School of Dundee, Dundee

The Loves Of My Life

Many things I have loved in my life:
Lying in a warm bed on stormy nights,
Listening to the ferocious howls outside.
Books with adventures filling every page.
Quiet mornings, bringing with them hopes for another day.
Still nights with friendly shadows hovering around,
To protect rather than frighten.
The sound of flutes, whose music is the wind's creation.
Wild flowers, smiling to the sun,
Dancing to the sounds of nature.
Fairy tales that light up a child's face
With a smile that sweeps away the day's tiredness.
Winter, the artist who decorates the world
With a soft white blanket.
To ice skate, flying over ice like a bird soaring through the sky.
Steaming mugs of chocolate that warms me up
After fights with the bitter cold.
Pillows, lots and lots of pillows,
Their softness cures all my pains.
To be high up on the mountains
Looking down at the Earth's vast beauties.
The last second of sunset
When the world plunges suddenly from brightness to darkness.
My teddy bear, my dear old friend,
Always there for me and me only.
Lastly,
My most precious possession,
A loving home.

Annie Ning (14)
High School of Dundee, Dundee

Called Up For War

I was with Elizabeth. She is my wife,
You see she hadn't thought of having kids.
Until she married me.
Our tenement was tiny, but it suited us four fine.
The rooms were always spotless.
Happy days.

And then we got the messages - I remember it so well
The radio beamed news across the land, 'We have entered into hell'
I had to sign up my name, I felt it was only fair
To serve my country till the end of the dreadful World War scare.

For six whole months I waited, I was really quite a wreck.
The names that were called up were put up in the town hall
Every day I went to check
Then one day my fear came true.

I was going off to war and I went outside and started to cry
I didn't care who saw, I went home an hour later.
My eyes were swollen and red.
My children carried on despite, but my wife had bowed her head.

I didn't want to go; I had to.
I bade my goodbyes to Rosie and Matthew
But Elizabeth looked at me with pain in her eyes
As the rain poured from the skies.

On the truck the guys were nervous
I could sense it in the air
Beads of sweat ran down their faces
Some were silent in prayer.

The thought entered my head that I might never be here again
As the wretched truck lumbered round the bend
And headed for the world's end.

RIP
Donald F McEwan
Missing in action; presumed dead
May he rest in peace.

Kirsty McEwan (12)
High School of Dundee, Dundee

Expressions

One cloudless, sunny morning,
As I strolled along the city street,
People's expressions were swarming,
Mixing with the summer day heat.

A suited man pushed past me in a hurry,
Just by one small glimpse without being obvious.
I guessed he was rich from that portly belly,
But a sleepless night just passed, all work, no telly.
Those sullen shadows haunted his sallow face,
Stealing the place of happiness in his life was worry.

Dodging the path of a starry-eyed lover,
Distant stare, dreamy smile and clumsy actions.
I wished it were me, what she thought, I have known,
Trapped in a bubble, a world of her own.
Being in love is a beautiful sensation,
Her feelings can never hide under cover.

Cheerfully racing against the school bell again,
Ranting and raving about last night's football game.
Not a worry in the world or a word about work,
The grinning faces cover the mischief that lurks.
Kicking and shouting with no one to blame
Brrring! The doors swing open and suck in the children.

A stick in her left hand and groceries in the other,
Past the wrinkles you can see the liveliness,
So much advice, so many tales to share,
But nobody listens, nobody cares.
She chatted away through her teeth, which were false,
That cosy smile that remained always with her.

Just by one little sneaky peek,
Of each face that passed me by,
I could tell of their troubles that week,
Expressions can't hide, they are not shy.

Rachael Sinclair (13)
High School of Dundee, Dundee

Feeling Is Believing

Things which mean the most to me:
The dancing smoke as you blow out a candle,
Its charred aroma mingling in the air.
Watching flames flickering and the tingling as the orange glow
reaches your skin.
A kindly, reassuring smile from a friend
and the tight embrace of a caring mother.
The Christmassy bouquet of red apples and oranges,
cloves and hot fruit punch.

Clear bubbles flowing downstream like sailing boats on the tide.
The smell of newly cut grass, whispering trees in the forest
and riding my bike in the rain.
Cold marble against the skin, musty rafters and cool autumn breezes.
The satisfied feeling as curled, crispy leaves crunch underfoot
And the lacy frost on silver, sleeping leaves.

The warmth from within as you laugh heartily
and the contentment after an inspiring conversation with a friend.
Colourful light shining through stained glass windows.
Beads of water draped across the spider's web
And the serenity of walking through an overgrown, forgotten garden.
The inner peace as I paint and the calm after a deep sigh.

Silence.
Watching moths and dragonflies flying low at dusk.
Cool, fresh linen on a close summer's evening.
The buzz as you receive a prize and being praised for achievements,
big or small.
Feeling the sun on your face and watching the shadows dance.
Hearing someone say, 'I love you.'
These experiences mean the most to me.

Victoria Sinclair Beat (14)
High School of Dundee, Dundee

The Loves Of My Life

The things I love:
The genuine smile of a stranger,
So unexpected and yet
A present full of happy feelings,
Its worth never known.

Heavy rain,
That makes your hair stick to your head
And your clothes to your body
And then the warmth rising off the pavement,
Sticky, clammy, smelling of summer.

The taste of chocolate,
When you're hungry and even thinking of it
Makes your mouth water,
Then when you eat it, it seems like the best chocolate
You've ever tasted.

Laughing so hard,
That your cheeks and tummy ache, and tears
Roll down your face,
How you just can't stop, and the more you try,
The harder it gets.

The way your hair,
Tastes of salt after walking along a beach,
When it's cold and really windy,
So windy it takes your breath away, but afterwards,
You feel clean and new.

Waking up,
To be greeted by a flawless blue sky,
And a cold sun,
The freshness of it telling you that today
Is going to be good.

Shona Watson (14)
High School of Dundee, Dundee

Life's Loves

These I have loved:
The dark shadows set by a fire
And the crisp, fresh, white of new linen;
The comforting feeling of my dog's head heavy in my lap
And the soft, velvet-like texture of her big floppy ears;
The smell of damp earth during the calm of a rainstorm;
And that first daffodil, so bright and so meek;
The time in the evening when shadows are long
And the sky is ablaze with orange and red,
Like some fiery battle in the heavens;
My kitten's heartbeat as she lies asleep on my chest,
Exhausted after hours of childish play;
The perfect touch of her gentle paw
And the deep motorised purr rolling from her throat;
The green bliss of my garden on a sunny day
And the soft tinkling giggle of a toddler;
The sweet tingly taste of a ripe blackberry,
I snatch before the sparrows do;
The calm of driving through grassy valleys so great and refreshing;
And the cosy comfort of my familiar car;
The cool of rain hitting my skin;
All the fiery, vibrant colours of the crispy autumn leaves,
As they fall so daintily from the trees still so strong, yet naked;
The thought of seeing friends so far away that each reunion is joyous;
Then there is the first morning you wake up
To find a blanket of snow smothering the landscape;
The glistening frost clinging to every branch and blade of grass;
Like a sparkling cocoon just waiting for spring to come
And open it up once more.
These I have loved.

Poppy Drummond (14)
High School of Dundee, Dundee

My Loves

The moist pink nose of a tiny kitten curled up on a soft bed,
Pine trees in winter, branches heavy with velvet snow,
Toasted marshmallows on a barbecue, brown with a crunchy shell
But with a feather-soft centre,
The feeling in the very pit of your stomach
As you plunge down a roller coaster,
Seeing friends after long summer holidays spent apart,
The sharp smell of burning leaves and branches
That nips your nose and throat,
Walking through a peaceful graveyard on a quiet, sunny day,
These have been my loves.

Watching old musicals and learning every word to every song,
Walking in crunchy autumn leaves wrapped up in woolly layers,
Having a long, luxurious bubble bath after a long day,
Taking a bow after a great performance in a packed theatre,
Scarlet rowan berries in the depth of winter, coated with silver frost,
The sheer exhilaration of winning a tough hockey match,
Elated and exhausted.
The taste of hot, greasy bacon rolls on a weekend morning,
These have been my loves.

Diving into a clear blue pool
After spending the morning in the baking sun,
Stepping through the revolving door into a cosy hotel lobby
After a long journey,
Decorating the Christmas tree with the same bruised and battered
decorations, year after year,
Feeling burning hot sand between my toes and the hot sun on my
back on a tropical holiday,
The decadent luxury of a New Year's celebration,
champagne and laughter and sparkling confetti,
All these have been my loves.

Caitlin McDonald (13)
High School of Dundee, Dundee

The Lone Skier

The sun rises gracefully and slowly,
Stretching lazily over the mountain peak,
Quietly beckoning,
Heavily laden white, snowy trees,
Glisten brightly on the icy slopes,
Quietly beckoning.

Zip, zip, zip, weaving neatly through the trees,
Wind gusting and rushing along the plain,
Pace quickening,
Whizz, whizz, whizz, going faster and faster still,
Torrents of cold air clawing and swirling,
Pace quickening.

The gully looms, lonely and perilous,
Enticing with its frightening, alluring charm,
Silently mocking.
Teetering nervously on the narrow edge,
The gully inviting, laughing triumphantly,
Silently mocking.

Zip, zip, zip, plunging downwards to its depths,
The gully taunts, swallows and sighs,
Deviously annoying.
Whizz, whizz, whizz, dropping further and further still,
The angry gully ferociously awaits more prey,
Deviously annoying.

The mountain rests, the lone skier reflects,
The day ends peacefully and happily,
Quietly receding.
The sun sets gradually behind the mountain peak,
Colours fade gently from yellow to red to blue,
Quietly receding.

Stuart Mires (13)
High School of Dundee, Dundee

Things I Love

I love to see a boat bobbing on the waves;
the delicacy of bubbles on a sunny day;
a smile from a stranger;
the bright, swirling patterns of fireworks in a dark blue sky;
to see stars delicately placed;
a hawk as it glides effortlessly through the clouds;
the fish as they hide from the herring;
the delicate rose filled with dew on a frosty morning;
the slim, elegant figure of a wine glass;
a rainbow in the sky,
the way light bounces off glitter;
the simpleness of a child;
castles on the Rhine
and the field mouse
as he weaves his way through the plants in my garden.
All these things I love to see.

I love to hear the chitter-chatter of my friends,
but also to hear the silence in the dead of night;
the sound of crisp snow under my boots;
the miaows of newborn kittens;
the laughter of a toddler;
the happy clanging of wedding bells;
the blackbird as he sings his song on the fence;
the crunch of leaves under the paws of a large, brown-eyed spaniel.
All these things I love to hear.

All these things I love to taste:
Italian pizza, a mouthful of Belgian chocolate,
a refreshing glass of apple juice;
a frothy hot chocolate, with marshmallows and cream
and the special taste of home-made food.
All these things I love to taste.

All these things I love to feel:
the thrill of a roller coaster;
the happiness you get at Christmas;
the cold snow on my face
when all the kids in my neighbourhood have a snowball fight;
the sympathy of a good friend;
daffodils dancing around my legs;
the freedom of running in the wind;
the excitement when a letter from a friend arrives
who has long since gone.
All these things I love to feel.

All these things I love to smell:
the mixture of fragrances in a wild meadow;
the particular aroma of Mum's cooking;
the stench of the pages in a new book;
the strong smell of red wood and the perfume of lavender.
All these things I love to smell.

Rachel Fraser (14)
High School of Dundee, Dundee

The Ghost In My House

All around the house he is moaning
In the garden he is groaning,
Through the bedroom he is swishing,
Round the bathroom he goes swooshing,
Round the kitchen he is growling,
Across the hall he goes prowling.
These are the sounds of the ghost in my house.

He is white as ever can be
Tall, much larger than me.
His eyes are bloodshot and red,
Skinny and thin, like he's never been fed.
He wanders about in the middle of the night,
Looking for humans who are out of sight.
These are the sights of the ghost in my house.

Katy Rodger (12)
High School of Dundee, Dundee

My Greatest Loves

These are my greatest loves . . .

The smell of fresh bread in the morning, lingering in the air,
The buzzing of the bees on a bright summer's morning,
Rainbows arcing through the blue sky,
The sound of children laughing and singing on their way home
from school.

Autumn leaves, rich in colour, floating down from the treetops on a
brisk autumn breeze,
Soft silky sheets and a warm bed after a hard day's work,
Home-made mince and tatties, on a cold winter's day,
Spreading warmth throughout my body,
The soft touch of my dogs' hair running through my fingers.

Fluffy white clouds floating through the sky,
The friendly orange glow emitted from towns and cities
During the long, dark winter nights,
The benison of hot water, when fully submerged,
And running water's dimpling laugh when meandering down to
the sea.

The satisfaction when people smile back at you,
The exhilaration of tearing open presents wrapped in paper
And wondering what's inside,
The haunting sound of the bagpipes,
Rays of sunshine bursting through the clouds for a marvellous effect.

Playing a game of cricket, with your friends, on a hot summer's day,
Helping my dad round the farm and spending some quality time
with him,
Sitting around the dinner table as a family, while having a roast dinner,
Laughing at my dog as he jumps up and down while we serve up
his breakfast.

Looking at my exam papers and realising that I have got very
good marks,
Turning on the radio and hearing my favourite song being played,
Receiving an unexpected letter in the post,
The last remaining drops of dew on colourful petals, glistening in
the morning sun.

Going on holiday and hoping that where you are going to is what
                                                          you expected,
Eating a greasy fish supper once in a while, but not too often,
Being able to sit out in the sun all day and read a book,
Mucking around on the bales, in the fields, with a couple of friends,
Dancing 'Strip The Willow' while trying to make your partner fall.

These are my greatest loves.

Adam Robertson (13)
High School of Dundee, Dundee

Some Things In Life

There are some things in life which cannot be bought or even lost.
There are some things in life that I love.

I have loved . . .
The crashing of waves on the sandy beach;
The tumbling of waterfalls against the stony river.

I have loved . . .
The zesty tang of lemons and limes;
The Christmas scent of cinnamon and pine.

I have loved . . .
The silky smooth coat of a tiny puppy;
The loving comfort of a huge bear hug.

I have loved . . .
The twinkling constellations of a moonlit night;
And the biblical rays of sunlight through thunderous clouds.

There are some things in life which cannot be bought or even lost.
There are some things in life that I love.

Rachel Clark (13)
High School of Dundee, Dundee

Down At The Graveyard . . .

. . . Phantoms frolic,
Coffins creak,
Wolves whisper,
Spirits speak . . .

. . . Witches cackle,
Monsters moan,
Tombstones tumble,
Gremlins groan . . .

. . . Wind whispers,
Mummies mumble,
Dogs howl,
Ghost grumble . . .

. . . Serpents slither,
Demons dance,
Am I staying?
Not a chance!

Fabliha Hussain (12)
High School of Dundee, Dundee

Across The Great Divide

An end to worldly troubles
Or
A beginning to a new existence?
A void of darkness, nothingness,
The fate of one and all that live.
Destiny: inescapable, inevitable,
No matter fortune, no matter fame
Calling all into the same.

Life, once bright is growing dim
He now calls the essence to him.
Extending a hand, a welcoming embrace
Accepting the death he now comes to face.

Erin Middleton (12)
High School of Dundee, Dundee

Hallowe'en

In yesteryear, on Hallowe'en,
The witches in their covens met,
To chant and sing and share their evil,
Huddled together, cold and wet.

A devil's curse indeed was present,
As a storm raged in fury all night,
A flash of lightning, a roar of thunder,
The noise of anger in full flight,
A place of vice and terror.

Witches, ghosts and bats today,
In gleeful groups they tramp around,
Throughout neighbourhoods lanterns shine,
As guisers they look and sound.

A feel-good factor and happy chatter,
As the joyful tricksters make their way,
To parties, friends and granny's house,
'Trick or treat?' they will say,
A time of fun and merriment.

Jennifer Grewar (13)
High School of Dundee, Dundee

Snow

The snow lies thick
Upon the grass.
A glittering carpet,
A silvery mass.
Like jewels embedded
In a cloth of velvet.
The world lies asleep
Under this wintry blanket.

Aisling Goodey (12)
High School of Dundee, Dundee

These That I Have Loved

Rupert Brooke is not the only lover, for I have loved too,
These are the things I love . . .
Starting a roaring fire;
The crisp smell the burning wood creates;
Minor key harmonies;
The crash of thunder and the flash of lightning;
The clean lines of a modern room;
The majestic soaring of an eagle;
The view of the treetops from my bedroom window;
And the noise they make when the wind blows.

There are a few quiet pleasures I still enjoy:
The sweet taste of fresh bread;
The strange smell of petrol;
A heavy bass line played loud;
The feeling of achievement when I finish a book;
The smoothness of new sheets;
Playing a song on the piano well;
The exhilaration I get when I reach the top of a hill.
I plan to add to this list as I go on -
These are the things that I love.

Tom Phillips (14)
High School of Dundee, Dundee

Seasons

Every year seasons come and go
Whether summer sun or winter snow.
The rain throughout blows to and fro
Every year seasons come and go.

Every year seasons come and go
Spring flowers, autumn showers
And the winter wind blows . . .
Every year seasons come and go.

Scott Ralston (12)
High School of Dundee, Dundee

Fire

It started small, just a couple of sparks,
But that was quite enough;
They went away and forgot about it,
That was a mistake.
It found another fuel source
And it spread about the room
Then started climbing up towards the roof.
It blazed throughout the household,
Wreaking havoc everywhere,
Its passage clearly marked.
Smoke rising high in the night sky gave the first warning,
But by then it was too late.
A loud rumbling followed by an enormous crash,
The house collapsed and fell to the ground,
Still burning brightly, along with everything left in it.

Alex Dolan (13)
High School of Dundee, Dundee

Growing Up

As each day goes by
I keep on growing up.
Every day I try and try
I cannot slow down the years.

Have my moody teenage years
Taken over my childhood joys?
Will I ever run or cheer,
Skipping along a sandy path?

When I grow older
Will I shudder and groan?
Will my heart shrivel and turn to stone?
Will I remember the joys and the pains?
Will I long to live my life again?

Jenni Hagan (13)
High School of Dundee, Dundee

The Things That I Love . . .

These are some of the things that I love:
The warm embrace of a comfortable bed;
Being indoors when a storm is raging outside;
Newly opened flowers dancing in a spring breeze;
The reassuring smell of my mum's cooking;
Chocolate, as it slowly melts in my mouth;
A comforting voice when I am upset;
And watching flames as they dance and leap in the hearth,
Without a care in the world.

The first warming rays of the sun on a quiet spring morning;
The smell after a rain shower has kissed life into the dry earth;
A deep breath of crisp air on a winter's morning;
Warm sand as it flows freely between my toes;
Looking down on the blanket of clouds from an aeroplane window,
As if you could reach out and touch the soft pillows below;
Laughter and happiness as it lights up a sorrowful face;
The simple joys of everyday life,
That makes it all worthwhile.

Christine Reid (14)
High School of Dundee, Dundee

My Great Loves

I love the smell of dark chocolate
When it hits my tongue.
And I love the taste of lemon juice
No matter where it's from.
The icy cold of winter's wind,
Winning a race and scoring a goal.

I love making someone smile,
The smell after it rains,
Opening gifts on Christmas Day,
Playing football in the rain.

All of these have been my loves,
But most of all, I love love.

Mark Pringle (13)
High School of Dundee, Dundee

The Hour The Skeletons Rattle

When the rain falls and the wind blows,
When the darkness overlooks the cattle,
When the Devil's trident swiftly rose,
That's the hour the skeletons rattle.

When the bats do fly,
When silence is broken by a witch's cackle,
When the wolves do cry,
That's the hour the skeletons rattle.

When you hear the eerie groan,
When voices in your head do prattle,
When you wish you were not alone,
That's the hour the skeletons rattle.

When pounding beats drum in your heart,
When nightmares end in a bloody battle,
When suddenly you wake with a start,
That's the hour the skeletons rattle.

Suzy Boath (12)
High School of Dundee, Dundee

Things I Love

I love being on my board and smelling petrol on the road as I pass
or being on the hockey pitch with the fast pace
and the sound of the ball cracking off the stick.
I love being at the bike track with the damp odour of crumbly earth
and the bubbling of the stream.
I love to go shooting and smell the powder burning after the shot.

I love the smell of wet dogs and the way the hairs stick to you.
I love it when good music comes on in films and there are good bike
chases and the rider gets away from the police.
I love the smell of burn outs and the roar of a speeding bike;
the hiss of paint as it leaves the can and the smell it has when it fills the
air, but most of all I love to sit in front of an open fire
and watch snow falling outside the window.

Stewart Darling (13)
High School of Dundee, Dundee

The Seasons

The seasons start with colourful spring,
Pink buds and newborn lambs.
The sense of new life everywhere
And on the breeze a scented calm.

Now we're at brilliant summer,
The time for sea and sand,
Where children laugh and splash and dash
Through the waters, hand in hand.

Next we come to rusty autumn,
When leaves begin to die.
But children still are skipping round
As falling leaves drift by.

Lastly we come to wolfish winter
Its bark as harsh as its bite!
But fun is still all around in the air
During a hard fought snowball fight!

Alistair Brown (13)
High School of Dundee, Dundee

The Ghost

One night in Weeping Willow wood
A boy named William went for a walk
All of a sudden he heard
A creaking, cracking sound,
Like footsteps on the old dried up leaves on the ground,
A figure of a man slowly glided out onto the path,
All of a sudden the man gave out,
A terrible shrieking scream
And it was then William realised,
This was no man
Or nothing of the human race,
At this point he realised that this glowing figure
Did not have a face.

Jonathan Irons (12)
High School of Dundee, Dundee

Angrily

Angrily the violent storm raged on
Angrily the driver tooted his horn
Angrily the protester tore down the sign
Angrily the girl gave him a piece of her mind.

Angrily the waves tore up the wood
Angrily the wasp stung the baby, hard as it could
Angry is the war - but angriest of all
The families of the victims who fall.

Maud Sampson (13)
High School of Dundee, Dundee

Jewels

If you've raided Mum's jewellery box you'll know what this is about;
Sparkling bracelets and twinkling rings,
Earrings and necklaces,
A ruby as red as a drop of blood,
Emeralds glinting as green as the leaves upon trees,
Each time they catch the light
A beam of sunshine shoots from each jewel.

If you've seen a coal mine before, you'll know what this is about;
Golden slivers desperately trying to shine through,
All the dust and dirt,
Gold as sparkly as glitter,
Silver as shiny as the stars,
When one digs them out, a small fortune is in one's hands.

If you've been in a jewellery shop before you'll know what this is about;
Glass cases everywhere containing precious jewels,
Sapphires as blue as the deepening night-time sky,
Opals as colourful as rainbows
And diamonds as clear as the crystals
Gleaming in the shop window.

Jenna Ballantyne (12)
Hunter High School, East Kilbride

The Rainbow Poem

Red is the colour
The colour of love,
Blood gushing from a cut
The flames it will rise above.

Yellow is the colour
The colour of the sun
A bright summer's day
When summer's just begun.

Pink is the colour
The colour of a bow
A lovely pink ribbon
In a ballerina show.

Green is the colour
The colour of the grass
You're out playing football
When you fall as you shout, 'Pass!'

Orange is the colour
The colour of a fruit
The bright car headlights
That flash to let you through.

Purple is the colour
On my lips the lipstick goes
Walking down the catwalk
Then you stop to strike a pose!

Blue is the colour
The colour of the sky
Where all the little bluebirds
Are flying way up high.

Cassie Rossiter (12)
Hunter High School, East Kilbride

Goodbye

I can still feel your fingers entwined with mine,
They fitted so perfectly.
I can still see your beautiful eyes,
Gazing into mine.
I can still hear the warmth in your voice,
When you said you loved me.

I understand you want to move on,
I understand you'll be happier without me,
But that won't make it easier to say,
That word.

Just one small word,
To make you happy,
To make me cry,
It hurts so much,
Goodbye.

Alice Gillham (15)
Invicta Grammar School, Maidstone

Unjust Pain

Nothing was heard on that most eerie night,
But the lonesome howling of the great white wolf.
All souls are gone, hiding, quaking with fright,
The thun'rous sound of his paws on the dirt.
Panting and moaning, he tosses his head,
A piercing shriek shatters the clear night's sky.
He winces with pain and lets out a whine,
He lies on his stomach, knows he will die.
Solemnly he ambles back to his den,
Bleeding, he recalls the bullet again.
His chest rises then falls for the last time,
He dies there, tired, bleeding and in pain.
To kill an animal of such pure grace,
The hunter found dead with blood on his face.

Emma Rippon (12)
Invicta Grammar School, Maidstone

The Sun

I am a giant fireball
Lying in the sky
Not a bird or bee has touched me
As the clouds go by.

And when the winter comes
I hide behind the clouds
They are my woolly blankets
As I stand looking proud.

I was here before all the rest
The sun, the moon and stars
And I will live for many years
Maybe longer than Mars.

Yes, I am powerful, I am great
And I am going to be
The greatest football ever created
In all of history.

Rachel Foreman (12)
Invicta Grammar School, Maidstone

Old Willow Way

Walking down Old Willow Way seemed strange at first,
As no one goes down there into the misty deep
Where the shadows walk, talk and creep
As a soul lies there with a broken heart,
Killed by a knife so thin, yet so sharp.
The man in life watched his daughters be slain,
He tried to protect them, alas in vain.
He succumbed to the knife and lay dead in the lane.
To stay there forever and suffer his pain.

Becky Holden (12)
Invicta Grammar School, Maidstone

Strawberries And Cream

Some people like them
Some people don't
Some people will eat them
Some people won't.

Some people like strawberries
Some people like cream
Some people like neither
Just the smell makes them scream.

Strawberries are juicy
Strawberries are ripe
Sometimes they're firm
And sometimes they're just right.

Now see I don't like strawberries
I don't like cream
But I wouldn't be nasty
Because that's just plain mean.

Jessica Lomas (12)
Invicta Grammar School, Maidstone

Limericks

There was an old lady from Kent
Who complained wherever she went
Last night on the bus
She made such a fuss
That complaining old lady from Kent.

There was an old man from Coxheath
Who ate toffee and out fell his teeth
He looked high and low
But the answer was no
That poor man could not find his teeth.

There was a lady who lived in a shoe
Who did not know what to do
The shoe stank
The smell was rank
So she started smelling too!

There was a blind man from Dundee
Who of course could not see
He walked into a tree
And thought, *what could this be?*
That non-seeing man of Dundee.

Poppy Tester (12)
Invicta Grammar School, Maidstone

The Spirit Of Christmas

The children of the opera sing
The heavenly church bells ring
The light of the day dims
The peaceful song of hymns.

The star is put on the tree
It's shining for everyone to see
In the baubles I see my face
The beads are shaped like lace.

As the family gathers around
Presents from the ceiling to the ground
As I look up to the sky
I'm trying not to be shy.

I decide to sit next to Nan
And then Uncle turns up in his van
My dinner comes out with Mum
Mum gives me a packet of gum.

My nan says, 'This is for you.'
It's a present, I say, 'Thank you.'
Family, I love them, I knew
At Christmas this is what you should do.

Emily Williams (11)
Invicta Grammar School, Maidstone

Biography Of One Singer

A magical thing happened in 1958
What could it be?
A magical singer was born
His parents full of glee.

He grew up with his 8 siblings
They loved him to bits
But when they make him angry
His eyes fell down to slits.

He was in a group with his brothers
They were called the Jackson 5
When they made world tours
Everyone wanted to see them live.

He soon broke up with his brothers
And went to a solo career
Then a dreadful thing happened
But people still loved him far and near.

He had vitiligo
At the age of 29
It doesn't hurt his reputation much
So I guess you could say he's fine.

As you know he's in a bit of a mess
And his reputation is going down the drain
And if he is proven guilty
It will give his fans a lot of pain.

You must have guessed his name by now
Michael Jackson is who he is
It doesn't matter how much you despise him
His songs you just cannot dismiss.

Jasmine Jakubuwski (12)
Invicta Grammar School, Maidstone

The Beast

The moon that shone brightly,
But was not to be seen,
Through the mist that lay lightly,
Over the graves on this night.

The church of this graveyard; still and cold,
The trees, dead and swaying,
And the graves all green with mould
And in the centre was the beast.

It was all hairy and damp,
On all-fours and panting,
It moved its paws with a quiet stamp,
Its teeth bloodthirsty and like giant thorns.

Its smell, so damp and vile,
Yet its body like a dog, but bigger,
With its own individual style,
Where it moves so cautiously.

As the smoky mist then parted
And the moon, the light from above shone,
The creature standing there started . . .
To howl, and howl and howl.

The beast with white teeth glistening,
Had moved its head back down
Stood there a while, looking and listening,
Before darting back and away.

It ran as quick as a shooting bullet,
To save its endangered life,
It didn't even stop to look back or sit,
It just ran, ran home to its cave.

Or did it?

Jessica White (12)
Invicta Grammar School, Maidstone

Autobiography In Five Chapters

I walk down the street,
There is a deep hole in the sidewalk,
I fall in.
I am lost . . . I am hopeless,
It isn't my fault,
It takes forever to find a way out.

I walk down the same street,
There is a deep hole in the sidewalk,
I pretend I don't see it.
I fall in again.
I can't believe I'm in the same place,
But it isn't my fault
It still takes a long time to get out.

I walk down the same street,
There is a deep hole in the sidewalk,
I see it is there,
I still fall in . . . it's a habit.
My eyes are open,
I know where I am,
It is my fault,
I get out immediately.

I walk down the same street,
There is a deep hole in the sidewalk,
I walk around it.

I walk down another street.

Katie Brown (14)
LACE Service, Halifax

Letter From A Box

Dear Love, my friend, long time no see
For stuck in this wretched box I be
That loathsome Zeus with his dirty tricks
Has locked me into this dreadful fix

And with such companions you wouldn't believe
The horror I'm going through you cannot conceive
I long for my kind and cheery friends
Instead the awful nightmare knows no end

Violence and war are as thick as thieves
They plot and they scheme their evil deeds
And when they get stuck for nasty ideas
They enlist the help of their evil peers

As for despair - he's driving me mad
His incessant groaning is making me sad
He mumbles and mutters his miserable groans
As he paces the walls with his creaking bones

After insisting all along we would surely be free
My moment finally came to make them all see
But instead of escaping when the box lid came off
They all went without me, the miserable lot

So here I am, all alone in this cell
Trying hard not to see it as a living hell
Do call me, pop in, stay for tea
It's really quite nice now that it's only me

Of course one day I'll surely be free . . . won't I?

Charlotte Coekin (12)
Lady Margaret School, London

Saint George And The Dragon

Why does everyone hate me?
I don't eat much,
I don't eat the sheep they send me,
I keep them in my backyard as pets.

I'm not bad really,
I was at the back of the line when they were handing out good looks.
It's not my fault really.
Why does everybody hate me?

Now they're sending me humans,
I keep them out the back with the sheep,
They're funny things really;
Keep thinking I'm going to eat them.

I may look fierce and horrible,
But don't judge a book by its cover,
I'm timid really,
The villagers just don't understand.

I wish I had something comfy to live in,
Not just this horrible cave.
It's dark and dingy,
I like cuddly and warm.

Just the other day you know,
This little girl was sent to me.
She was wearing a little gold crown.
She didn't want to come in.

Then this guy came in,
How dare he? Thinking he can come uninvited.
Wearing a red cross on his chest
And all that armour on too.

I hate it when they wear armour,
It looks so silly,
It doesn't go with the furniture,
And ruins the carpet.

Well, he came in and stabbed me,
I pretended to lay down dead,
He took the princess by the hand,
And led her down the road.

All I could hear was cheering
'The dragon is dead
Hooray for Saint George.'
Saint George . . . who's he?

Laura Turner (12)
Lady Margaret School, London

A Small Box
(Based on the legend 'Pandora's Box')

Who would have thought such a small box could hold so much;
The burdens of the world in a case.
Six thin walls withhold the terrors within
But not for long, I know; Pandora will soon give in.

Unknown terrors will cover the world;
War, death and pain.
A picture-perfect vision of cruelty.
Hope kept under lock and key.

Then the greed of both human and beast
Enough will not suffice;
A wealthy man and famished child,
No creature undefiled.

The freedom of life without hurt and pain
Will soon be thrown away
When chaos and havoc will roam the earth
We'll soon see what curiosity is worth.

Beatrix Lovell-Viggers (12)
Lady Margaret School, London

Odysseus' Sister

If I throw one stone, you would throw one further.
If I sang one note, you would sing one higher.
If I ran one marathon, you would run two.
Our parents knew you would be bigger, better than me.
They knew you would be taller, stronger than me.
They paid all their attention to you, but never any to me.
All the time I saved your back, you never gave me any slack.

You had craftsman's hands and a lover's heart.
Seven years you fought Cyclops, lotus flowers and the sirens' songs.
For seven years you were gone.
All the adventures you had made me sad because I never got to go.
If I had gone, men would have thought it bad luck
To have a woman on board.
Just a woman's luck, even though I was best at the sword.

Now that we are all grown up and the child's bickering has stopped
I've done the one thing that you could never do,
I've named my son after you.

Julia Huettner (12)
Lady Margaret School, London

I Wonder . . .

I wonder what came over me,
The day I went to go and see
The waterfall, so fresh and bright
Oh! What a breathtaking sight.
Suddenly, out of the blue,
A pixie came and took my shoe,
A little fellow, full of delight
Put him in my pocket, I might.
He ran and ran out on the road
Carrying my heavy load.
I gasped and chased after the being,
I could not believe what I was seeing.
All of a sudden, he snuggled into my shoe,
And you just can't help but love him too.

Marleena Cronvall (13)
Lymm High School, Lymm

Friendship

We used to be best friends
All those years together
Just like sisters
When you went away
Part of me went with you
Now you've come back
I no longer know you
You've become a different person
I wish I could rewind time
And make everything right
If only you could be the person
I used to know
Why did you waste your life
On these people?
They've messed around with your head
You think you're cool, but you're not
I can't handle this anymore
Soon you'll regret what you've done.

Natasha Ogilvie (13)
Mid Yell Junior High School, Shetland

Death

When life begins,
It's all so happy,
We live so long,
But when the time comes
We have to go,
We don't want it we know,
Because death, death, death, is a horrible thing we know.
So be careful to live so long and happy
And don't do drugs and don't do drink
Because if you do I can say you won't live long and happy.

Tanya Marie Finnie (13)
Mid Yell Junior High School, Shetland

Racism Is . . .

Racism is a very bad thing,
It splits up families, communities,
Kills people, and divides the world.
Racism is a roaring monster,
It eats people alive,
Killing them without mercy.
Racism is a rally car,
Churning through the WRC of life,
Messing up the tracks
If we could stop racism,
The world would be a better place,
Less fighting, less conflict,
Less hate and less anger,
If we could only stop racism!

JJ Smiles (13)
Mid Yell Junior High School, Shetland

Death

Death can be slow or fast or bad,
Death can be something very sad,
Death can be bloody,
Death can be sore,
Death is like opening one giant door,
It's only a plunge,
It's only a fall,
It's only some time,
Till you're not there at all
And when you finally realise,
That you are dead,
Your life is just a faint memory,
Inside your head.

Merryn Jane Tonner (13)
Mid Yell Junior High School, Shetland

Always Together

A lways and forever
L oving you is easy
W aves of love I can't describe
A nd thoughts of you are in my mind
Y es, I love you day and night
S ongs of love running through my mind

T ogether forever I wish we could be
O n and on my love is for you
G oing crazy thinking of you
E ndless love I have for you
T onight I wish we could be together
H earing your voice sends shivers down my spine
E verlasting love is what I have for you
R unning through my mind you always are
                and you always will be.

Zandra Williamson (13)
Mid Yell Junior High School, Shetland

Love Is All Around

Love can make you happy
Love can make you sad
Love may come
And love may go
Making you happy
Or leaving you sad
Love is all around us
So take your chance
And give your love.
I would like this war to stop
And spread my love
To the people in Iraq.

Kerry Reanne Nicholson (13)
Mid Yell Junior High School, Shetland

Love

Every time I see you
My heart is pounding,
I wait outside,
I really wish I had a date.
No one likes me,
Everyone hates me,
Except you.
You smile at me
And I smile back.

Stephanie Caroline Keith (12)
Mid Yell Junior High School, Shetland

Depressed

Depressed and lonely,
Sad and separated,
You think you'll get better,
But you won't,
Not after what you did,
Taking drugs wasn't the solution!

Jack Jamieson (13)
Mid Yell Junior High School, Shetland

Life

Scared and tired
Thinking about life.
Sitting in his bedroom
Thinking about life
Going outside
Still scared and angry
Feeling very lonely
And so tired.

Sophie Lamb (13)
Mid Yell Junior High School, Shetland

Life

Life, you weave through,
And jump . . .
And then you fall right down
To the bottom of a pit.
You scramble to try
To get up from the muddy depths,
But never succeed.
What do you do?
Sit there and do nothing?
No, you try and try again,
Till you get to the top
And then life is yours,
To weave and jump through,
Once more.

Emma Coleman (13)
Northease Manor School, Rodmell

Sonnet

The soldiers who had guns were yet to cease,
The battlefield was covered in red blood,
The war over and the world is at peace,
The blood that was turned into wondrous buds,
The buds that were turned into flowers fresh,
The poppies that were fresh were deeply loved,
The soldiers who had died were deeply missed,
The families did pray to Heaven above,
The news had reached them that their loves were dead,
The relations were grieving and in pain,
The anniversary was once a year,
The memory of loved ones had come back,
The battlefield was covered in red blood,
The blood that was turned into wondrous buds.

Anna Willis (12)
Onslow St Audrey's School, Hatfield

Haiku

Sunflower awakes
Stretching high up in the sky
Looking for the sun.

Stephanie Masvodza (11)
Onslow St Audrey's School, Hatfield

My Happiness

I walked through the garden,
All coloured with flowers,
Tulips, pansies and roses,
I could stare at them for hours.

As I proceeded through the garden,
I came to a halt,
I pulled a twisted face,
It was like I'd eaten salt.

Rats, mice and spiders,
Were going through my mind,
As I anxiously wondered,
What it was I'd find.

My face returned to brightness,
Brighter than before,
For what I saw was . . .
A pile of puppies lying on the floor.

This garden I've been walking through,
Show some things that make me happy,
Flowers, puppies, family,
And poems that are sappy!

Micha Jayne Thompson (12)
Perth High School, Perth

Human Nature

When we're born
We're not the same
Whether we're cute,
Small, strong or lame
To our mum we're the perfect being
The greatest picture
She could be seeing.

When we're four
We live a life
Of fun and games and of no strife
Girls play princesses
Boys, soldiers with guns
Cos when we're small, all war is fun.

When at school
We work and learn
Or mess about right through the term
What we're taught will mould our life
Our job, our house
Our husband or wife.

When we're thirty
It's hit or miss
The rest of our life has led to this
Let us hope
Our life is fine
All bad feelings are in decline.

When we're old
Has our life
Been worth the effort
Worth the strife?
Have we found love or fear or fame?
Cos we've got one shot, then we're all the same.

Lachlan Gillies (12)
Perth High School, Perth

Death

He's lying there with nothing to do,
Waiting for the obvious to come true.

Every moment more pain, every second less strength,
If his time were in string, it would be a short length.

In a moment he's gone and so is his pain,
Never will I see his smile again.

He just slipped away, like fingers through sand,
He wanted us to enjoy life, that was his only demand.

I never had a chance to tell him how I feel,
But after that day death became so real.

One day, which I hope won't come too soon,
I'll see him again in light of both sun and moon.

Kayleigh Maud (13)
Perth High School, Perth

The Grim Reaper!

He stalks the streets in time of pain,
Going down every road and lane.
He looks at me with those deep-set eyes,
Glowing, shining, they tell no lies.
That permanent grin,
Says quite plainly, 'You cannot win.'
Why does he carry the harvesting tool?
It makes him look a complete fool.
He is definitely male,
Even though he is extremely pale.
That black robe clings to him like a creeper.
Who is he? He is my old friend: the 'Grim Reaper'.

Iain Ness (13)
Perth High School, Perth

Manchester United

With Howard in the sticks
And Ronaldo with his flicks
Ruud will provide the goals
As long as Lehman is between the poles

The new teenage prodigy
Wayne Rooney
Makes the most of every opportunity

Big Rio at the back
Will be keeping an eye on Henry
There is no doubt about that

Giggsy, Smithy and Saha too
Can rip right through the Arsenal crew
Last year Keano lifted the FA Cup
Thanks to Arsenal's big muck-up

Yes, of course, this is the wonderful Man U!

Matt Burbridge (13)
Perth High School, Perth

The Violin

The violin lay cradled in her arms
The bow glided over the strings
The notes soared into the velvet night
Riding on the whispering wind.

In the heavens above, the stars twinkled
The moon gave his soft, slow smile
And on the Earth the crowd stood enthralled
As the notes entered their hearts.

Then at last it stopped
The night was still
Then came the roaring applause!

Kirsty Hazelton (13)
Perth High School, Perth

In A Dark Place . . .

We approach the abandoned house with care
Doing this really just for a dare
Empty it had stood for many a year
These days no one goes so near.

We push open the door, it makes a loud creak
Into the hall we quietly sneak
Dust and cobwebs lie everywhere
We bravely start to climb the stair.

We reach the top, we think we see blood
Perhaps not, it's only mud!
Then we hear an angry voice
We look around, we have no choice.

Eyes are black, yellow teeth and must be nearly seven feet tall
Scratched and bruised, he's been in a brawl
We turn and run down for the door
I catch my foot and hit the floor.

I feel his hand and I try to scream
I open my eyes, it was just a dream.

Christopher Ewing (12)
Perth High School, Perth

View From A Window

As I look through the glass
I see different cars pass.
I see trees on the hill
And up the road, ruins of an old mill.
I see birds flying about
And living in the river are trout.
Leaves scattered around
Some in a mound.
The cold air has a bite
But the view from the window is a beautiful sight!

Katie Malloy (12)
Perth High School, Perth

The Death

It was silent
It was violent
One slash of a knife
That was it
His life was over.

He lay there for days
Up on the hill
He had friends and loved ones
But still no one realised
The missing man - was dead!

A kid was walking
Saw the body
Stood staring
Not knowing what to think.

A sudden scream
Running down the hill
Looking for someone to help
No one was around.

A week later the funeral came
The body was at peace
But the girl wasn't
Her scar was there for life.

Rhona Donaldson (13)
Perth High School, Perth

Trapped In Love

She moves through her life
And he is holding her
His words fill her mind
But she never sees him
They are lost in an eternal embrace
For they are held in love
But torn by death.

Camrie Hole (13)
Perth High School, Perth

War

In war there are no heroes,
There is only the brutal hack and slash of swords,
Good men die,
Bad men live,
And yet it still goes on,
Where is the heroism in war?
All there is is blood and death,
There is no good or evil,
Only men.

Ross Hunter (13)
Perth High School, Perth

Malky

In through the cat flap he came,
In his mouth a small creature, shocked and lame
But the horrendously overweight beast
Was not entitled to this feast
And both animals were thrown out the door
Where one landed dead and one pretended to be sore
The small rodent lay on the grass
And was torn apart by the immense, grey mass
A fat cat!

Seán Kennedy (13)
Perth High School, Perth

Poet For Today

Sitting on the shelves,
The authors by themselves,
J K Rowling, Phillip Pullman,
Roald Dahl and co,
Fantasy, mystery, horror and more,
Fiction, fact and information,
All will capture your imagination.

Casey Martin
Perth High School, Perth

The Reality Of Christmas

Shepherds following a deep, shining light,
Baubles and tinsel, gaudy and bright,
No room at the inn, only the stable
Crackers and turkey set on the table.

Baby Jesus sleeping sound,
Money for presents, pound after pound.
Wise men arriving to worship the King,
Children planning what Santa will bring.

Angels surrounding, beginning to pray,
Peacefully celebrating the real Christmas Day.
Not one full of shopping, presents and food,
But rejoicing Christ's birthday,
Like all of us should!

Rosie Christie (13)
Perth High School, Perth

Fall

I suppose you know, as a matter of course
That gravity works when you're riding a horse
If he suddenly goes forward with a thundering sound
The route you are taking tends to lead to the ground.

I suppose you would know, as a matter of course
The sound waves work when you're riding a horse
On the showjumping round, if he baulks at the jumps
You'll usually land with a series of thumps.

So think before you make up your mind
And think before you bend down behind
Or you may carry forever the print of his kind.

Amber Martin (12)
Perth High School, Perth

Titanic

Two lovers, who are meant to be together
Separated from each other by a marriage
Their love is strong, but is it strong enough
To give them the power to become one?

They wait for the right time
But will there ever be one?
They ask themselves, what is there to lose?
The answer is everything, yet nothing.

How did love get so complicated?
No one knows
You must seize your opportunity
Before it is too late.

Nicole Bright (13)
Perth High School, Perth

My Cat

My cat is as black as a dark night,
He stares with great big orange eyes,
Shining like the stars,
Always alert for what could be a surprise.
He sleeps all day without a stir,
At night he wakes with rippling fur,
He chases mice,
And rabbits and voles.
He is not fond of great big dogs,
As they often chase him.
But at the end of the day he's got a soft heart,
And I love my cat, Whisper, the way he is.

Anna Taylor (12)
Perth High School, Perth

Broken Home

His mum and dad have split up,
This broken home has messed him up.
His mind is now full of woe,
He's like a child, lost in the snow.

Twelve years they were together,
For better, for worse, for whatever.
He thinks that his life has been a lie,
He's even wished that his parents would die

So that he could get them back,
For the pain, the grief, the straw that broke the camel's back.
Life now seems empty,
His mind is full of self-pity.

A new life he wishes he could lead,
His father's main sin was greed.
And his mother's was a loveless marriage,
Their life came apart like the wheels off a carriage.

He wishes that life were back the same,
So that there was no divorce to mess up his brain.
The anger that built up inside,
Was silenced by his inner-child.

His mum and dad have split up,
This broken home has messed him up.
His mind is now full of woe,
He's like a child, lost in the snow . . .

Mark Mitchell (13)
Perth High School, Perth

My Sis

My sister and I don't get on
She thinks she is right
But really she is wrong.
We always argue over silly little things
And of course she always wins.
I'm sure Mum and Dad like her best
God knows why, I think she is a pest!
Apart from that I know deep inside I shouldn't curse
Because, after all, it could be much worse.

Rebecca McCann (12)
Perth High School, Perth

The Sea

Like a wolf the sea can howl
Like a bird it sings a song
Like a tiger on the prowl
Sometimes crashing on the rocks.

Watch the foaming waves at night
You will see its wild horses
Playing in the white moonlight
Seeming quite fierce but really tame

When it lets the children play
The sea will once again feel free
It shows its gentle kind ways
When they leave, it feels so sad

Listen to its whistling song
The sea - beautiful but sad
Takes you out, it is so strong
And like a songbird it sings.

Sian Denning (11)
Royal High School, Bath

My Day

I wake to the morning sun,
Knowing that it will be another day of fun.
I jump out of bed and down to the kitchen to be fed.
I make my breakfast and eat,
And run to my lunchbox and sneak in a treat
And then back to my bedroom on my heavy size 6 feet.
I look in my wardrobe, wondering what to wear,
When my brother of doom sneaks into my room.
I then go to school,
Hopefully looking cool.
I go into the hall,
Hoping not to fall.

The day is over and I'm going home,
Hoping my friends will give me a phone.
I get home and play with my friend Cath,
And then step into a warm, cosy bath.
I go in the lounge and see that my brother is watching TV,
I walk off seeing that nothing interests me.
I go to the kitchen to be fed,
And then walk off to bed, my legs feeling like lead.

Jessica Watters (11)
St Gerard's School Trust, Bangor

The Sun

Bright blazing ball of fire,
If you get up close it will make you sizzle.

It's up there now looking down at us,
No flicker of movement, no orbit.

Every other planet circles around it,
Is it a planet or is it a star?

It provides us with heat and light on Earth,
One half at a time is daylight.

Higher than the Earth, the moon and the stars,
And as big as Elvis!

Each day scientists find out more and more about it
Through telescopes and satellites.

But in a couple of thousand years,
It will blow up!

Benjamin Hughes (11)
St Gerard's School Trust, Bangor

The Sunlight

The sun shining so bright
Reaches out with its massive
Light.
So high in the sky but still in
Sight.
A huge fireball too hot to fight.

Jack William Stanmore (11)
St Gerard's School Trust, Bangor

A Growing Question

Along the wall of life, the boys do stand,
Football, cricket bat and bike in hand.
Sports shorts, trainers and baseball caps,
Their greatest skill, some believe, is reading maps.

Along the mall the girls do walk,
Make-up, fashion and boy, do they talk!
Shopping, chatting and silly giggles,
On the dance floor their silly wiggles.

Along the road of life we learn and see,
That everything is not what it seems to be.
Girls are silly and boys are dirty,
So why do they all grow up and get flirty?

Alex Brown (11)
St Gerard's School Trust, Bangor

What's Missing?

The most popular girl in the school.
She has long hair and everyone thinks she's cool.
Her name is Chloe, but nobody did see how sad she was inside.
Every night she would cry and wish that the days would go by.

What's missing? She wonders, looking out of the window,
Like a minnow, trapped behind glass.

All she needs is to be cared for, and not to be shut
Behind locked doors

Stacey Jane Palmer (12)
St Ives School, St Ives

So You Like Metaphors?

So you like metaphors, huh?
Okay, then let's play.

She was beautiful, not to them but everything to me
Her long neck, slender body, which just begged to be gripped,
Seemed to call to me as port does to a ship
It didn't really matter what label she wore
For in her sparkling depths was the compassion I sought.

In her, I knew, was something murky lurking,
But nevertheless, she seemed to impress,
My now transparent mind, now distant, smirking.
She never was the answer to my problems and probably presented
                                            me with some herself,
But whilst in her presence life's issues I forgot,
Without her, the purpose seemed defeated, fatal pain its cost.
Unfortunately this is not the tone of love's tale,
The bitter-sweet goodbyes always turn soon to stale.
For without this treat, of which I consumed in the most amazing
                                            of feats,
My days turned to pink elephants running frantically.

That didn't rhyme, did it? Well, that was supposed to shock.
In the best poetic tone I will continue to mock.

We went joyriding, without a seatbelt,
In her parents' room, our bodies collided,
But yet, apparently, it was not *my* accident.
My best friend's carelessness was to blame.

Blood, known as life's juice, right?
If so, life flows from his cold, motionless throat.
I remember slipping on life when I left him.
Yep, life is wonderful!

Peter Marezana (16)
St Joseph's Academy, London

The Girl At The Window

The girl at the window
Is special as you say
She lives in a world
Of terror and dismay

She wants to be happy
She wants to be kind
She wants to live her own life
And rule her own mind

The person she longed for
For years and a day
Cut himself free
From the terror and dismay

His blood makes her curtains
His life makes her walls
His heart in her heart
His soul in her floors

This war is wrong
But it shall not end
This war shall be fought
To the very end.

Jessica Elliott (12)
South Wirral High School, Wirral

The Phoenix Bird

The phoenix bird makes me think of life
and how mine is not so nice.
The phoenix bird is big and strong
and how I feel so alone and so weak.

The phoenix bird is beautiful and bright
but my life is so dull and dark.
The phoenix bird has a perfect life.
Maybe one day I will have a life
like the phoenix bird.

Tanya Citrine (13)
South Wirral High School, Wirral

Equus

The cavalry canter majestically
On a dust-swept Horse Guards' parade,
Far away from past epochs where
They made charges and reckless raids.

Under Rameses they dragged great chariots
Under Alexander they harassed the flanks
In medieval days they were valiant knights
With armour, a shield and lance.

Seventeenth century brought Oliver Cromwell
And his Ironsides in the Civil War
Disciplined and tenacious
Thund'ring 'cross misty moors

With Napoleon, cavalry blossomed
Into immortal exotic beasts
From his roving rash Hussars,
To his Mamelukes from the East.

But in the snows of Russia their myth decayed,
And shattered at Waterloo
Where the Redcoats stood immovable
Against seas of green and blue.

Down a shell-strewn valley charge the Light Brigade
Gaudy heroes of the Crimean War
Blue-clad warriors hacking with sabres at
Startled Russians, crouching in awe.

Onto audacious German Uhlans
In patrols sprawling through the plains
Inciting panic and paranoia
From Metz to the River Seine.

But four decades on these noble steeds
Met the epilogue in poppy fields
Machine guns and mortars blew them away
And so hooves were replaced by wheels

Of grand and daring cavalry though
Memories still endure
That enterprising free spirit which
Changed the face of war.

Daniel Tyler (14)
South Wirral High School, Wirral

Phoenix

As I rise from the ashes
A burnt city lies beneath me
The air is filled with smoke
The wind wraps me in a cooling blanket
I hear nothing, just silence

The souls of the people who have just died
Are rising up towards me
Help is on its way but it's all too late
All that is left now are the eerie, charred remains
Of what was once a beautiful city

But do not mourn too long
As this city is Phoenix
And will rise again.

Danny Ashworth (11)
South Wirral High School, Wirral

Let Me Out!

I am in a street,
A busy street,
There are many people,
There are many faces,
There is not a body to be seen,
None, nowhere,
I am confused,
I don't know where I am,
I panic,
I sweat,
'Let me out!' I scream and scream,
No one can hear me,
All the faces gather together,
They stretch and squirm,
I can't move,
I want to run away,
I want to rip through the people and run home,
But no,
I can't move,
I yell and scream,
I tug and pull,
Until finally it ends,
And I'm wrapped in my quilt.

Lucy Vaughan (11)
South Wirral High School, Wirral

The Phoenix Poem

Noises were heard from every direction
as the phoenix rose from the ashes,
crackling sparks filled the sky.

Smoke towering into the air blocking out the sun.
Its roar echoing throughout the forest.

Fire set alight around the trees.
Fiery breath shot out of the bird's mouth.

Its beady eyes sparkled in the blaze;
the creature's wings flapped,
blending with the colours of the fire.

Its magnificent colours of red, blue,
yellow and green became camouflage.

The phoenix feeling joyful began squawking
burning hot . . . hot enough to burn a forest.

Its super-sized wings made everything feel so small.

The phoenix so beautiful and magnificent
set off into the distance . . .

Sam Jones (11)
South Wirral High School, Wirral

Why?

Looking out the window,
Wondering why,
Why him?
What did he do?
Why did he have to die?
Sitting there quietly,
Water dropping from her eyes,
What would she do if someone else dies?

Richard Davies (12)
South Wirral High School, Wirral

The Dying Sunset

Silence was all that was to be heard
Until . . .
The wind blew the lush green grass
Fresh air touched my face.
I watched the sunset fade and the sand flicked in my eyes.
I saw a luminous orange tree anchored in the sand.
The wood on it was deep and hollow
It was getting eaten
Eaten by
The swirling sand and shingle
But . . .
Everything changed
Sand turned to dust
Grass turned to hills
The sand changed colour
This strange orange tree stood still flickering in the last of
                                        the sunset's light
When the sunset's light dies, so will the tree.

John Jones (11)
South Wirral High School, Wirral

Prayer

Dear God,
Please don't let him go
Please don't let him slide into your loving arms
Or be at your right hand

Or be in your gentle care
He must stay here to help me
He must stay here through my trouble
My flight of pain
My time of need.

        Amen.

Holly Chrishop (12)
South Wirral High School, Wirral

Bullies

So alone in my secret room,
I hope I'll be accompanied very soon.
Clouds creep past in the night,
Darkness and mist give me a fright.
Owls hoot as they flap their wings,
They are lucky, they can't feel these things.
Bullies laugh and cheer as my arm breaks,
They don't realise their nasty mistakes.
Coldness and chills make me freeze,
On my bare face, I feel the breeze.
Window slams shut, I sit on my bed,
I need to sort out the mess in my head.
What did I do? It's not fair,
My so-called friends don't even care.
They push me around in school,
Acting as if they are really cool.
I'm definitely not going to class tomorrow,
All I feel is pain and sorrow.
The anger builds up in my head,
I don't want to be here, I'd rather be dead.
I hope the bullies feel my pain,
Some day I hope they will feel the same.

Amy Louise Down (14)
South Wirral High School, Wirral

Woman Waiting For Her Destiny

When her love is dying
She is the one who is crying
Wind blowing in her face
Clouds thundering in her place
Locked in her room
Waiting for her love to come soon
Hair throwing itself all over the room
She is waiting for her destiny.

Liam Forrest (12)
South Wirral High School, Wirral

The Lady In The Window

The lady in the window,
Why is she sitting there?
Is it a dark and gloomy day?
Maybe she's just upset.
The girl just sitting there,
Her mum and dad have died.
She is planning on getting married soon.
Maybe she's thinking it's all too soon.
Does she really love him?
She loved her mum and dad.
Should she marry him?
What happens if he dies too?
Would she ever be able to go outside again?
Maybe even speak to people
Would she be dead, depressed, die herself
Like her family has just done?

Matthew Drew (12)
South Wirral High School, Wirral

The Window

As I look out of the window
I see the dark night's sky
I see the stars, they're really bright
And I begin to cry
Why am I alone now?
Why do I have to pray?
I wish I had a bunch of mates
I could play with all day.
The truth is they all left me
And went out without me
But if I keep speaking to God
I might hopefully break free.

Joel McCann (12)
South Wirral High School, Wirral

So Upset

I'm sitting in my room so upset
The rain splashes on my face, so cold,
As cold as ice
I think how much I love you
How much you hurt me when you left
I need you back
I really need you back so much
I want you back
Don't you love me anymore?
I love you so much
How could you leave me?
You need me and I need you too
So come back, come back,
I love you so much.

Imogen Merrick (12)
South Wirral High School, Wirral

The Brittle Tree

The sky is blood,
Like a red, roaring fire.
The naked branches, all bare and brittle.
Is it in a hot place?
Is it autumn?
Is it just the sunset?
The lonely tree swaying in every piece of breeze,
So thin and brittle.
Will it snap?
If it does, when
And why?

It could happen!

Gemma Murray (11)
South Wirral High School, Wirral

The Phoenix

Here I sit in the school entrance,
On show for all to see.

What am I hearing?
Elves arguing, phones ringing and people talking.

What am I seeing?
Elves beneath me, flames surrounding me
And people rushing by.

What can I smell?
Smoke and school dinners.

What can I taste?
My fiery breath.

How am I feeling?
Sad and scared, does anybody care?

Emma Bonett (11)
South Wirral High School, Wirral

The Phoenix

Those people running.
Their fate in the phoenix's hands.
Some flying, some running.
Each and every one of them
Could die tonight
On the sand.
The phoenix is dangerous
To every one of these creatures.
The phoenix's eyes are one of his deadly features.
The phoenix is deadly.
Moving across the beach steadily.
Tears of poison
To kill you with.

Mathew Purcell-Jones (12)
South Wirral High School, Wirral

Flames Of A Phoenix

Flames slash my feathers,
I'm christened with the ash.
The crackling fire starts to quiver,
And burn the golden grass.

Eyes open a fiery red,
My life comes from what was dead,
My heart is free and I will fly,
High into the icy sky.

The air cuts through.
My feathers burn true.
I spread my wings and fly,
Darkness cowers at these mysterious powers,
And flames eat the sparkling sky.

The fire burns down,
Darkness pours in,
My heart begins to drown,
I shall fall to the Earth,
To the place of my birth,
And my soul is burnt right down.

Ben Davies (13)
South Wirral High School, Wirral

Broken Heart

You really, really hurt me
I don't know what to do
I cover my face to hide my tears
I will never ever forgive you.
Why did you do this?
It drives me mad
Just thinking of you
Makes me so sad.

Becky Green (12)
South Wirral High School, Wirral

Inside

As I walk with a deceitfully designed smile disguising my face,
Inside my heart is painfully parting,
Being torn apart by every emotion.
Uncontrollable feelings race towards the surface,
I press them back down for my own personal purpose.
Affection wants to spill out,
But delicate gates lock in my tears.
On the outside I look happy, as I powerfully pace towards
                                              my destination.
My legs lead me proudly,
Inside my body is quaking, shaking with apprehension,
I want to crash to the ground.
Now I am here, I stare down,
Hundreds of feet above the concrete.
Graceful tears glide down my colourless cheeks,
My legs tremble as I shakily take one more step,
Which to me is a giant leap.
Still wearing a smile,
My body, happily slams to the ground,
There is nothing inside now.

Heather Jones (15)
South Wirral High School, Wirral

At The Window

I am sitting at the window all alone
No one here to make me smile
My special person has gone away
He was meant to be back three years ago
I think he might be dead
But I am not sure
The thunder and the rain are making me scared
But it's showing me how I feel
Still looking out of the window
Waiting for my someone to return.

Amy Goddard (12)
South Wirral High School, Wirral

The Lonely Girl

I sit in the window
Watching the dreadful storm
The rain falling heavily from the dark cloudy sky
Watching the wind blowing the trees so hard
Thinking, *why is the weather so cold?*
The sound of the planes going past.
Sitting in my room all alone
No one to keep me company
No one to keep me happy
I hear the wind rushing through the air
Feeling like crying as much as the rain

So scared
So scared!

Rebecca Cross (12)
South Wirral High School, Wirral

The Hand In The Sand!

The crashing waves, the cold seas,
My hand is stuck, so help me please.
Twisting black roots are pulling me down,
Grab my hand before I drown!
The green hills are growing,
No, it's just me sinking,
I'll lift myself out, that's what I'm thinking.
I can't stretch, I've tried and tried,
I've stretched until muscles hurt inside.
The tide is too close,
There is no point now,
Just let me go, I'm too far down!

Sophie Hughes (14)
South Wirral High School, Wirral

By The Window

By the window she stands, every day,
Crying, crying,
She knew her mum was dying
Looking down on the street below
Taking a deep breath and
Sighing, sighing
Crying, crying
Her mum was about to die
Turning around
She frowned
Her mum was no longer there
She didn't quite know where
But she had gone.
Looking out of the window again
Crying, crying
To the people below
It felt like rain
She will never see her mum again.

Charlotte Murray (13)
South Wirral High School, Wirral

Looking Out The Window

The window is shiny and cold
The girl is not even that old
She is gazing out of the window
Because she has become a widow

She is missing her loved one
She can see his ghost when she daydreams
She can also hear his screams
When she goes to bed, the day ends.

Carol Colquhoun (12)
South Wirral High School, Wirral

The Sea

I can hear the crashing of the sea lapping up against the bedrock,
The seagulls' flight, the flapping wings compliment the silence,
I can feel her sorrows and bitterness towards the sea,
As it blasts her with an icy blow.

The wind continues blowing, carrying the aroma of the flowers
                                                        all around,
And sending the smoke from the kettle towards her telling her
                                                        it's ready,

Before she wanders into the warmth of the house,
She glares back at the place, the ship, her loss.

I can see her mourning, I can see her,
For I am only a mere shadow of her past,
I still bear the saltiness of the sea,
Dragging me under until there is no hope.

James Shell (12)
South Wirral High School, Wirral

War

War is all over the place
I think that it's a disgrace
But when it's on a game
It is not the same
But in real life it is just a shame
As the bullets are flying, people are dying
Families are crying all over the world
But military isn't the only type of war
There are gangster wars out on the streets
As they're cruising around listening to proper beats
Guns are firing
People are dying
Why is there *war*? It should be no more!

Joshua Phillips (13)
South Wirral High School, Wirral

The Different Culture Rug

The 'different culture' rug.
With two young people standing tall.
The woman trying not to see the dripping blood,
Which the deadly army underneath has done.
Pictures all around, all about their life.
The 'different culture' rug, that's where we live as life.

The 'different culture' rug,
As the gunshot shoots,
Then the lady cries,
With the water wailing, as the bird tweets.
Pictures all around all about their life.
The 'different culture' rug, that's where we live as life.

The 'different culture' rug,
As the blood drips down her body.
I can almost taste everything
The murky water, this dusty rug.
Pictures all around, all about their life.
The 'different culture' rug, that's where we live as life.

Heather Rankin (11)
South Wirral High School, Wirral

The Palm Tree

*T*he teenager hidden
s*he* stands behind a palm tree
her family may have lost her.

*P*robably they should go back
*a*s she hides behind a tree
*l*ater they find her alone by a
pal*m* tree.

*T*here she'd prayed quietly
the*re* she was scared
she stood there like she saw a ghost
her family to her home to where she belonged.

Kate Patterson (13)
South Wirral High School, Wirral

The Four Towers

The clear bright blue sky
With the air bouncing clouds
The birds drifting in the air singing a song to themselves
The bells ringing
People singing happily themselves as they rejoice about a
                                            newborn baby

Four large towers scratching the blue sky
One white, one beige and two dark, deep shadows
No one in the street but me
The patterns on the windows, one like a giant daisy from a giant
The windows are clean like a crystal

As I look up all I can see is the beautiful sky
While down below the feet is a cobbled path
Half-grey, half-broken, some cobbles kicked out
All the buildings are rough
But one brick is smooth like sandstone

The smell is beautiful
Freshly baked bread that has just come out of the oven
The smell of fresh air
Nothing is going on, all is silent
The feelings of happiness you can feel all around you.

Lisa Moore (12)
South Wirral High School, Wirral

Leaves

Trees breezy in the fresh air
Infants eating and playing everywhere
Old men eating mints and playing chess
Gangs making the old park look a mess
Rubbish blowing far and near
Leaves rustling on the ground
People looking at the graves
People making loud noises
But in the end this park is going
To be here for years to come
Maybe in centuries to come
Your grandchildren will be here too

Sophie Dawson (13)
South Wirral High School, Wirral

Alone

Alone on my own, no one there,
Lost in nothingness
How did I fall into this trap?
How long have I left to survive?
I feel nothing more than the grit and sand
Why can't salt taste of sugar?
Why can't I have a chance to escape?
Why do I have to feel lonely?
I haven't deserved this!

Hannah Davies (13)
South Wirral High School, Wirral

Help Me!

What are they doing?
Why are they there?
I want to be free,
I should be out there,
I've done nothing wrong,
They are my friends,
I need them to hear,
But nobody can come up here,
Shouting them to come and help me,
Am up here all alone,
I need to call but there's no phone,
Maybe I should smash a window,
Where is my family?
Are they OK?
Are they in the crowd out there?
Hopefully they're looking for me,
Soon I will be found and free.

Georgina Treadwell (13)
South Wirral High School, Wirral

All Alone

I've tried to hide the scars on my face.
I'm sitting here alone in the empty room.
You left me here, gone without a trace.
It feels like I've been left in an empty tomb.
I am crying for help but no one can hear me.
Who am I?
I'm so completely confused.
I don't know what to do or who to see.
I am so scared.
I am badly abused.
Will someone please come and help me?

Sai Howes (13)
South Wirral High School, Wirral

The Warriors Are Coming

I hear the screams of children and adults alike,
Running through the grass trying to break free,
I hear chanting of the beating drum,
The warriors are coming,
The forest is set alight,
I feel the tortured souls racing in the air,
The leaves of the trees falling, falling, falling,
For every leaf that falls, another life is taken,
I see blood on the trees,
Blood on the leaves,
I see lifeless bodies just lying in the cold,
The warriors have been where life has been,
And now they have gone there is no life to be carried on.

Lauren Clyne (15)
South Wirral High School, Wirral

Ashes To Ashes

Ashes to ashes,
Dust to dust,
No matter how many bashes,
I'm not very fussed.
I'm yellow, orange and red,
Remember I'll never be dead.
Ashes to ashes,
Dust to dust.
I'm loyal,
Praise me I'm royal.
Don't get on the wrong side of me,
Or you will pay the fee.
Ashes to ashes.

Sarah Holden (13)
South Wirral High School, Wirral

The Local

The church bells ring, as the people gather round,
Everyone excited for the church service,
As people walk into the church they each give a pound,
Feelings throughout everyone who is there.

The shouting of the people gets louder and louder,
Children start to scream and run about,
The service is near to beginning,
And the church starts to fill.

Feel of the two buildings as they rush past,
And the feeling of the banner that lies ahead,
Everyone starts to move quite fast,
As the church bells start to ding and ding.

The smell of the other people was horrid,
So was the smell of bad crisps that had been left there.
The service begins and people start to quieten down,
Crowds of people getting smaller and smaller.

The church fills up and the service starts,
The town part empties while the service is on.
Only town around,
Which is called 'the local'.

Sarah Jones (12)
South Wirral High School, Wirral

The Phoenix's Hope

The smoke was thick black,
Ashes from a long gone fire were exploding,
From every burst ash a soul appeared to regain a new life again,
A mighty roar suddenly arose from beneath the ground,
Then, as if from nowhere, *a phoenix rose* up from the dead ashes,
It was luminous red, yellow and full of new hope.
New hope that would be sent to everyone and everything,
He knew he was free and he could do anything, go anywhere,
At any time.

Peter Shell (11)
South Wirral High School, Wirral

The Last Soul Of Earth

As the war for Earth begins,
The sky turns blood-red with fire.
Evil invades mankind's territory,
Everything cremated into dust
A single tree left standing
Could this be the last soul on Earth?
The tree placed between good and evil,
As the battle begins.
Raindrops crash into the ground like bombs,
Trying to extinguish the flames.
Blood rushes through the ground
Staining everything in its path.
The tree is the only living thing
In this new pit of Hell.
The tree remains alive whilst burning
In the new pit of Hell
This tree is the last soul of Earth
Forever burning, never to be put out.

Stuart Mackenzie (14)
South Wirral High School, Wirral

The Phoenix

Evil is fleeing
When it sees my being
Rising above the dark
My bright flames will lead the way
For any soul who might stray
Back into the dark
When you hear my cry
You know evil will soon die
Because I
Am the Phoenix!

Sam Busby (13)
South Wirral High School, Wirral

Autumn Leaves

Autumn leaves are falling to the ground,
As summer slowly drifts away,
The trees are now getting bald
But what will see them through each day?

The flowers that grew in spring and summer
Are rotting in the paths,
As the beautiful petals and leaves
Slowly turn to dust.

Children collecting conkers,
With leaves rustling under their feet,
Making them brown and mouldy,
But it will soon be clear again.

Autumn is almost over,
Winter will soon be here,
The branches will turn to frost
And the ground, white and clear.

Alexandra Ellen Moss (11)
South Wirral High School, Wirral

Dream

The night sky
Wolves breathing on my neck
A shooting star
A heavenly place to be
Warm slippers on my feet
People talking
Cold rush down my spine
Clouds all around me
Stars glistening in the sky
Lightning hitting the ground
This is the place for me.

Andrew Thompson (12)
South Wirral High School, Wirral

The Blanket Of Dreams!

Lying on the blanket of dreams,
All you can see are the eggs cooking,
The sausages burning,
The fish flipping,
The people dancing,
The birds singing,

Lying on the blanket of dreams,
All you can hear are the birds singing
The eggs sizzling,
The people tap dancing,

Lying on the blanket of dreams,
All you can taste are the gorgeous sausages,
The yolk of an egg,
The birds eating worms,
The people drinking the fruity juice,

Lying on the blanket of dreams,
All you can feel or touch are the eggs burning in my mouth,
The sausages burning in his hands,
Stroking the birds fair,

Lying on the blanket of dreams,
All you can smell are the sausages burning
The people's perfume,
The fish frying.

Rebecca Edwards (11)
South Wirral High School, Wirral

The Phoenix

A new flame in a burning fire
The beginning of a life
Strength pumping into every vein
Rising into the sky
Feeling on top of the world.

Jack Ithell (12)
South Wirral High School, Wirral

Staring

Eyes of horror staring,
Watching through the night,
They shine very bright,
They watch your every move,
They are secretive,
You can see pain deep within them,
They look like they are crying tears
Cascading from turned eyes,
Black holes taking all their happiness,
Destroying them one by one,
Taking their memories,
Tormenting them,
Eyes of horror staring,
Watching through the night.

Michael Williams (11)
South Wirral High School, Wirral

Elegant Goddess

She sits as she's being painted
Elegant and graceful
Blue, pink, yellow, purple and green.

The painter is in love with a goddess
He captures the beautiful face
She sits for ages waiting and waiting
For her portrait to be finished.

As she's being painted
She feels unknown boredom
But!
Not to her knowledge
The painted portrait
The painter will cherish forever.

Robyn Eccleston (11)
South Wirral High School, Wirral

Presidential Election

When I woke I was confident,
When I was changed, I was nervous,
And when I was out there I was scared.

When I woke I lay in bed,
Thinking about this day,
I hoped today would go slowly,
So I waited where I lay.

When I was changed and ready,
I heard my name being chanted,
As I walked towards the amazing atmosphere,
I huffed, puffed and panted.

When I was speaking to the crowds,
My legs were wobbly as jelly,
I tried to keep my confidence with me,
But I remembered I was on the telly.

Sam Stewart (11)
South Wirral High School, Wirral

The Parting

The waves crashing against the ship
The sound banging in my ears.
The ship beginning to fade
Into the mist or is it the tears in my eyes?
The wind blowing in my face
The chill making me cold all over
The tears dripping down my face and into my mouth.
My skirt blowing against my legs
The sweet smell of the flowers
Mixing with the smell of the salty sea.
The man of my dreams fading into the distance
The picture of his face fading from my mind.

Yvonne Stewart (12)
South Wirral High School, Wirral

The Burning Bush

In a war-torn country
The tree burns.
The blood of innocent victims
Fills the sky and turns it red,
The colour of fire.
The tree dies
As it loses its leaves
It starts to crumble
And the ashes form a pile in the dust

A small child runs from
This decrepit land but then
A small piece of metal
Flies through the air
And hits him on the head
He falls to the ground dead!
Jack Powell (13)
South Wirral High School, Wirral

He's Gone

He has gone,
I hope not for long.
No one is here,
I can only feel the trickling of a tear,
I'm now all alone,
My husband isn't at home,
He's left me for a woman with fame,
I'm sitting by the window looking at the rain.
Why did he have to lie?
He could have at least said goodbye,
I don't know what I did wrong
But he has gone.
Kerry Ly (13)
South Wirral High School, Wirral

Skulls

I lie here for so long,
When I left my family they said, 'Be strong.'
I wonder and wonder
Will the weather ever turn to thunder?
Will I see the rain
Never again?
All I see is the sun
But I'm too weak to run,
For days we fought,
No fish I caught,
Someone realises I'm gone.
The water has gone,
The stars appear, they shine so bright,
Just like a garden light.
Not too light, not too dark,
I wish I was back with my kids in the park.

Zoe Russell-Baugh (11)
South Wirral High School, Wirral

The Burning Bush

B urnt to a crisp,
U nsteady roots,
R oaring fire in the sky,
N o leaves,
I magination sketches a picture,
N utrition scarce,
G reenery gone.

B urning rapidly,
U nbearably hot,
S carce water,
H and is reminiscent of a bush.

Lee Russell (11)
South Wirral High School, Wirral

The Eyes

They are always watching
Never listening
They can't listen because they are eyes
Everywhere you go they are there
The eyes
So many eyes
Some covered in fire just like blood
Some are like X-rays of your own eyes
Pale and white
Some as yellow as the sun
They can be brown like mud
No one knows where they have come from
Who do they belong to?
Different eyes give you different feelings
You can hear the voices of souls in the eyes
The souls of the past
The deep past
You will never see two of the same eyes at the same time
Beware of the eyes, the floating eyes and their dark souls.

Scott Gibson (12)
South Wirral High School, Wirral

The Worried Man

He watches a programme in the pitch-black,
His spine tingles down his back,
With hair standing on end,
Terrified and white.

He hears the screams of the ghost's fright,
With a haunted house, with an extreme height,
The programme was only one hour,
But now he can't sleep,
He can still hear the screams and ghosts,
All stuck in his head.

Sam Chan (11)
South Wirral High School, Wirral

Panic!

On my own now,
    it's hard to breathe,
        inhale, exhale, inhale, exhale.

Look in the mirror,
    reflection looks back,
        with eyes too bright,
            and skin too pale.

Sit back down on my bed,
    feeling dizzy, can't concentrate,
        my sweaty hands press upon my head.

Pull myself together,
    I can't be late,
        can't act like this in front of my mates.

No one understands,
    no one can know,
        how I react when I'm feeling low.

Stacey Moran (13)
South Wirral High School, Wirral

The Woods In Autumn!

As the brown crispy leaves crunch beneath my feet,
I get tangled in the overgrown ivy,
I look around to see the juicy berries hanging in the tree,
Looking around again to see what I can really see
Branches snapping, pine cones cracking,
Flowers falling all around my feet.
Autumn, autumn,
Leaves are falling,
Yellow, brown, orange,
Red ones too!

Zoe Kilpatrick (12)
South Wirral High School, Wirral

Swampy Seaside

Down by the seaside,
It's all swampy and green,
There's a man drowning,
And nobody's seen.

It's a tragic moment,
In this man's life,
It's a terrible feeling,
He's lost his wife.

He's feeling so blue,
Down by the seaside,
Nobody knows,
He's committed suicide.

His wife had no idea,
That her husband had died,
And when she found out,
Of course she cried.

She rushed to the beach,
To find her true love,
She saw him lying,
And looked up above.

She started praying,
To save him so,
But then she knew
She had to go.

Daniel John Owen (12)
South Wirral High School, Wirral

Skulls And Bones

What will happen to me?
Where am I?
How long will I last?
Lost in the desert with no supplies,
Mouth drying,
Body weakening,
In need of liquid,
Seeing mirages,
Lost in the desert with no supplies,
No living things in sight,
Forehead drenched with sweat,
Flesh burning,
Can't do anything to stop it,
Lost in the desert with no supplies,
How I wish for a gust of wind,
A sudden downpour,
The sun's rays are streaming down
No clouds to cover them,
A sandstorm's brewing!
Death hangs over me,
Lost in the desert with no supplies,
Will someone save me?
Will they ever find me?
Will they take advantage of me?
No life, just barren land,
Lost in the desert with no supplies.

Michael Higgins (11)
South Wirral High School, Wirral

Mother And Child

Sitting together
Protected
By the warm firelight
Feeling lonely
Only mother and child
Where's the father
To keep them safe?
Selfish
Maybe or maybe not
Not caring but only himself
Not the mother and child
What is he thinking now?
Regretting
The thought of leaving
Running away
Abandoning mother and child
Leaving them with the warm, bright fire
Tired
Child feeling sleepy
Mother looking worried
About the child with no dad
What are they going to do now?
Thinking
Thinking about the past
By just sitting in the dark
Lonely
Lonely together
Lonely together, being mother and child.

Deborah Liu (14)
South Wirral High School, Wirral

A Day In The Life Of Miss X

It was just a bit of fun
He grabbed my arms,
I knew something wasn't right
I asked him to get off me
But he didn't.
He then persisted to squeeze my arms
More and more
I froze as I realised
I knew what was going to happen after that

I told him to get off me
I told him he was hurting me
I told him to leave me alone
I told him I didn't want to
I told him I would scream

I started to wriggle
I thought it would help
Make a difference
He didn't move
He just stared at me,
All I could see was his face.

I started to feel completely helpless
I started to realise then,
Whatever I did
Whatever I said,
It wasn't going to stop him.

In the end I turned my face
And just cried the whole time,
Now it has happened
I keep thinking I could have done more.

When he finally got off me
I felt really dirty and cheap
I felt responsible
I felt I could have stopped it.
I felt so helpless just lying there
And all I could do was cry
I've never been so scared
In my whole life.

Kelly McEntee (14)
The College High School, Erdington

The Giraffe

Tall and proud,
They stand up high
And look over the jungle,
What can they see?
Lions hunting,
Cubs playing
Monkeys swinging
Elephants eating.

They walk gracefully
Through the jungle
Like a model
On a catwalk,
Their heads up high
As they pose elegantly
A smile on their face
As they reach their destination!

Hayley Kitch (12)
The Community School of Auchterarder, Auchterarder

The Elephant

A growl like an earthquake
Trembles through the ground
Things start to shake
No one makes a sound.

Until one breaks the silence
A trumpeting sound
The beast walks towards me
I turn slowly around . . .

This beast looms enormous
With giant grey ears
Tusks gleam in the sunlight
I start to fear.

Then with its long trunk
It tickles my ear
And I step closer
Forgetting all my fear.

Christina Davidson (11)
The Community School of Auchterarder, Auchterarder

Leopard

Lying low and stealthy in the grass
As it watches its prey, it lets time pass
Its prey are gazelles, shy and small
Not aware of the danger they're in at all
Soon it will take off as fast as light
But it's waiting until the time is right . . .

Matthew Anderson (12)
The Community School of Auchterarder, Auchterarder

Extremes

Africa is the place of lions,
Africa is the place of sun,
Africa is a place of no water,
Africa's where people want fun.

Iceland is the place of penguins,
Iceland is the place of snow,
Iceland is the place of icy water,
Iceland's where the sun shines low.

Scotland is the place of midges,
Scotland is the place of rain,
Scotland is the place of cold breezes,
Scotland's where people won't come again.

Claire Sneddon (11)
The Community School of Auchterarder, Auchterarder

The Elephant

Huge, dry, flapping ears,
Giant wrinkly toes,
Long blunt ivory tusks
And a funny-looking nose!

Powerful munching jaws,
Long swaying tail,
As it walks along the ground,
Great footprints mark his trail.

Slender dirty trunk,
Dark beady eyes,
Scares away predators,
With its great and mighty size.

Sarah Langlands (12)
The Community School of Auchterarder, Auchterarder

Nana

Nana was born 1922
But by the time I met her she was hardly the child she used to be.
She was quite old and frail.
But what happened to the memories of the places she used to know so well?
What about Baxter Park Terrace? The place she used to live.
Who is living there now and is it still the same?

What about the wedding picture?
Is that the same old Nana that I knew, dressed up in her little bridesmaid outfit?
Who are the other people, the beautiful bride and the handsome groom?
What was she feeling on that day?
Was she happy, sad or bored?
She certainly looks it.

And those happy pictures before World War II, did she know it was coming?
Did she like being a teenager in Scotland in the 1930s?
It was certainly different from nowadays.
Who was her friend?
What was her name and what was the name of her cute little doggie?
What about the picture of when she was fourteen?
Is it the back garden of Baxter Park Terrace that she is standing in?
Who is the man, is he a friend of the family or is he a member of the family that I never knew?

Then in 1939 the war came and Nana was signed up to be a land girl.
Did she want to be a land girl?
Did she feel good that she was giving a helping hand with the war effort?
But then, when I look closely at the picture I see a cigarette poised in her hand.
Little did she know that one day she would have to give up her beloved cigarettes forever.

Now Nana is gone and all of those happy memories too.
It was the cigarettes that killed her, gave her lung cancer.
Back in the 1930s she didn't know any better and by the time she did it was too late. The damage was done.
What about all those questions that I will never be able to ask, that Nana will never be able to answer?
I can only wonder.

Ailsa Dann (12)
The Community School of Auchterarder, Auchterarder

Nana

Is that me sat there
Smiling sweetly?
There's my sister with her cheeky grin,
Same clothes and hair,
My nana looking down on me,
I wonder what she is saying?

The smell that would always greet me
When I stepped in the doorway,
Running down the long and endless corridor
Looking for Nana,
Knocking on the heavy door
Waiting for my nana's hug.

Even though she has gone now
The perfume she wore still lingers,
I still remember her long beads
Draped around her neck,
Her hugs I remember
As if it was yesterday.

The photo will always be treasured,
And my nana never forgotten.

Anne McPhillimy (12)
The Community School of Auchterarder, Auchterarder

The Little Boy That Once Was Me

I was five, I was happy, I only cared about my race,
Me with many others, running slow and fast.
Never ever thinking, no expressions on my face,
I just hoped and hoped my best that I wouldn't come last.

For days and days I practised using up all my spare time,
But why, but why, wasn't it only a game?
I tried ever so hard, to ensure the race was mine,
Even now, I still think, *wasn't that so lame?*

Everyone around me, cheering different people on,
The golf ball on the spoon, the spoon made out of tin.
We were trying so hard, everything had suddenly gone,
But in our little hearts there was only one thing we wanted to do . . .

We wanted to win!

Daniel Ghamgosar (13)
The Community School of Auchterarder, Auchterarder

Then And Now

Far, far away from any civilisation is that place,
That so very long ago the stairs and grandness of the
Entry hall was welcoming.

Where once, every room was bright and gleaming
In the diamond-covered ceiling and the golden fleur-de-lys
Pattern of the carpets and the brilliant burgundy colour
Halfway up the wall, where servants were always kept busy.

Where now there are wet, rotting beams and a dark, gloomy courtyard
Enjoying the quiet and subtle silence.
The whispering of the wind through the shadowy corridors.
The darkness consuming the dusty, lifeless corners and cracks.

Zack Fummey (11)
The Community School of Auchterarder, Auchterarder

Gruesome, Gory Hallowe'en

A scary clown,
With black hair, skulls and crossbones on it.
Spiky teeth and blue lips
Red cat's eyes.
Wolf hands, sharp claws
Big clown feet.

Old raggedy clown clothes,
Eyeball buttonholes.
The clown can walk and talk only slowly.
He comes out at night,
Stays until three,
Waits in the night to give someone a fright.

Greg McArthur (11)
The Community School of Auchterarder, Auchterarder

The Lizard

It lazes in the sunshine
Where it's warm and dry
It stares at you boldly
With its little beady eye.

It can slither and crawl,
It can run; it can climb
Some look like they're covered in grime.

When it's time for dinner,
It sits with hungry mouth
And if it sees a bug
Then its tongue *pops* out!

Kris Grimes (12)
The Community School of Auchterarder, Auchterarder

Lord Of The Land

The lion roams the land
The dusty, dry savannah
He is lord of the land
And nobody disputes it

The lion feels hungry
He goes for a deadly kill
With a raging leap and bite
The antelope falls to its grave

The lion feels threatened
It will take a manly gulp
And with a mouth the size of Jupiter
Shout an angry roar

The lion doesn't like the opposition
It will charge at the unlucky one
With claws as sharp as scythes
It will give the opposition a beating

The lion roams the land
The dusty, dry savannah
He is the lord of the land
And nobody disputes it.

Ben Warrington (12)
The Community School of Auchterarder, Auchterarder

Birthday Treat

Disneyland, Paris, for my birthday,
My little sister's too.
Mum, Dad, my little sister and I,
Enjoying the sights and sounds.

Lots of pinks and blues,
Pink flowers and fairy tale castle too.
Roofs, railing and lamp post,
All coloured blue.

Mickey and Minnie in their house,
Sleeping Beauty in her castle.
Fantasy and fiction,
The whole way through.

Weather not great,
Didn't dampen our spirits.
Flat shoes definitely needed,
So far to walk, so much to see.

Back to reality all too soon,
It was time to go home.
That was the best birthday
Ever!

Patricia Mennie (13)
The Community School of Auchterarder, Auchterarder

The Tyrannosaur

The tyrannosaur hunts for its prey
Every night and day
It wakes up in the morning hungry
For its prey
It walks around looking for
Meat all day
He strikes fear into his foes
He's hungry all day
Looking for his prey
He's a killing machine
Every night and day
He's hunting for his prey
Every night and day
Then he gets his prey
Every night and day
When he's done with his meal
He goes away
When the time comes
When he passes away
It's time for the other predators
To eat him.

Martin Slamon (11)
The Community School of Auchterarder, Auchterarder

My Xbox

My Xbox is the best
It makes my square eyes red
But when I play my Xbox
It's more like a play box

I'll play another game
For when my old one gets lame
And I'll play it all night
Until my square eyes go blind.

Marc Hill (11)
The Community School of Auchterarder, Auchterarder

Gran

Who was to know?
I didn't,
The doctors didn't.
It was a shock
And we weren't prepared.
She was gone,
And we would never see her again.
At first I didn't understand,
Gone,
Forever?
Mum and Dad got to see her before she left us.
We didn't get the chance.

Mairi Urquhart (12)
The Community School of Auchterarder, Auchterarder

In The Winter

In the winter
When the snowflakes fall
All the children come out and play in it all

In the winter's night
When you look through the window
All you see is white and a little robin in the moonlight

The next morning
We go outside and all the snow is gone
So that is the end of my poem but most importantly, winter.

Ryan Miller (12)
The Community School of Auchterarder, Auchterarder

My 6th Birthday

I look at the photo in front of me
Is that really me smiling back
Celebrating my 6th birthday?

My eyes are fixed on the camera
There is no noise,
I am sitting silently,
Waiting . . . waiting . . . *flash!*
The flash blinds me,
I keep smiling anyway,
Just in case there is another flash to come.
There is not.

My eyes become clearer,
I am still sitting,
Waiting for instructions to move again.

Everyone starts talking and laughing,
The noise returns to its normal level.
I remember my gran smiling proudly,
My great gran just sitting and laughing,
My brother sitting quietly eating cake,
No recollection of the photo.

Yet here it is now,
7 years later,
Lying in my hand.

A happy day full of happy memories.

Roslyn Andrews (13)
The Community School of Auchterarder, Auchterarder

My Two Little Brothers

On my right, a photo
A young boy smiling,
A gap replacing a tooth.
The blond, brown hair
Flopping down, innocently
Into deep brown eyes,
Twinkling like little stars
In a moonlit sky.
That happy little person,
Full of life and energy,
Looking like butter wouldn't melt.
Never caring, never knowing,
Of the photo on his left.

On my left, a photo
A baby lying,
The cries never coming
From the mouth that stayed open.
A little white hat
Covered the delicate features
Of a bruised and fragile head.
The little eyes that would never open,
Never see the grief.
The tiny ears that seem unreal,
Never hearing the silence around him.
That little person, that little soul
At peace.

Charlie McArthur (13)
The Community School of Auchterarder, Auchterarder

Grandma

I was young, happy, free to explore
I had no worries
I didn't have to think about things

My sister, she was grumpy, upset,
Screaming and shouting

Grandma
Always happy, never sad
Always there for us

There was total
Silence

Not a word, then there was the loud
Flash!

For a few seconds there was total blindness
And then light was back

And now, here is the photo in my hands
I realise why this photo had to be taken that day
They knew what was happening
They knew that the day after the photo was taken
Grandma would say goodbye
For the last time

The end of an era.

Thomas MacLaren (13)
The Community School of Auchterarder, Auchterarder

My Firsts

My first time on a plane.
The engines roared,
I grabbed the arms of the chair,
The plane took off.

Looking down from 38,000 feet
Watching a film on the screen
Eating some rubbery plane food
The plane landed.

My first time abroad.
The sky was pure blue,
The hot weather advanced in around me,
There were new smells in the air.

The hotel was huge
The people spoke in a strange way
The sand on the beach burned my feet
The sea went on forever.

My first time when I was disappointed to leave.
We packed our bags
Checked out of the hotel
And slowly walked out to the taxi as we said goodbye.

We were onto the plane
I looked down at Spain
I was thrown back in my chair.
The plane landed.

Sam Mailer (13)
The Community School of Auchterarder, Auchterarder

Abe

I got my dog four years ago
It was a very happy moment
It was a surprise
Everyone came to my house to see him
He was just a puppy
He came with the name Abe
He was excited to see new people
The first time I saw him he growled at me

One day, I left my Game Boy lying on the couch
I went outside to play
When I came back he had chewed it to pieces
And sometimes he used to empty the bin

In my photograph, he is waiting to be fed
Once, my mum forgot to tell me he had been fed
Before she went to work
I fed him and he didn't eat his food
My dad and I thought there was something wrong with him
We took him to the vet and the vet said he was just full
That was a worrying time until my mum told us he had been fed
Then we had a laugh about it

Since we have had Abe I have had more priorities
I like to take him for walks and feed him
He knows when you are happy or upset
And knows when to lick your hand.

Jaqueline Hayburn (13)
The Community School of Auchterarder, Auchterarder

Photograph Day

Shaken awake early, scrubbed thoroughly the night before
Shoved into clothes, clean and ironed, fresh smell
Climb down dark stairs sleepily, into warm, cosy kitchen
Mother buzzing around like a bee on duty
Father reading newspaper like a slow, calm tortoise
Rush to sit down, food shovelled down throat at top speed,
nearly choking
Mother brings out comb and tames wild hair until scalps are
scraped and aching
Shoes tied and buttoned up, coats slipped on and front door opened
Pushed out into cold, misty morning, shoes clip-clopping on the
stone step
After at least five minutes, Mother and Father appear and lock the
small, wooden door
Marched down the street, Mother panicking unless we are two
minutes late
Cold wind blowing on cheeks, distance hidden by mist,
appearing slowly
Finally arriving, gloves knocking on door, small man with glasses
and moustache appears, rush of warm air
Stumble in, wiping feet on small doormat, coats and hats disappear,
told to come inside
Hustled into large room with grand furniture, baby starts whimpering,
taken out to calm down
Told where to stand, ties and ribbons neatened, bodies moulded
into shape
Baby appears, calmed now, is placed into mould with the rest
Photographer is happy, disappears behind camera, everyone ready
Click!

Jenny Hutton (13)
The Community School of Auchterarder, Auchterarder

My Puppy 'Patch'

When he came through the door at Christmas,
I stared him in the eye.
Joy gleamed on my face.
We were in love.
'Patch' was his name,
With his black and white spots.
His bottom slid from side to side,
When he was scared, nervous.
His lovely heart-shaped spots shone in the sun,
Like a butterfly's wings fluttering in the sky . . .

His beady eyes stare at me.
It's a dog show tomorrow,
He gets groomed and bathed,
Until he is spotlessly clean.

It's the next day,
We're ready to go in.
We enter in the 'most handsome dog' class,
But surely we don't have a chance.
The other dogs are gorgeous,
I just hope we get placed.
We walk around one by one,
And then the judges call us in.
Wait, I was wrong, we're, we're
Second, yeah!
He truly is the most handsome dog!

He's changed my life forever,
Brought joy and happiness to the family.
He sleeps on my bed at night,
I read a story to him.
He falls asleep like a baby angel up in Heaven,
Flying in the clouds with snow-white wings.
Nothing bad in his way, just the snow-white heavens.

Gemma Hughan (13)
The Community School of Auchterarder, Auchterarder

Hamish

A dark night
Rain padding against the window
Everyone round my kitchen table
Waiting, waiting
Waiting anxiously
He came in

Hours, minutes
And even seconds
Had passed with Hamish
He was quite shaggy-looking
Deep blue eyes staring right at me
He was tiny
Looking at us
Wonder what he was thinking
He was looking around the house
He had found his new home

Months and days
Minutes and seconds
Had passed with Hamish
Going out and playing with him
Sneaking him scraps from the table
Teaching him tricks
He wasn't very obedient
Running out the door every time someone answered it
Making lots of noise while we were watching the television
Leaving a trail of mess everywhere he went

Months, days
Minutes, seconds
Everyone gathered in the garden
This birthday had come so quick
The flames were blaring on the barbecue
Dad coming out with a cake and a candle for him
Looking back on it all
With the photo in my hand
Hamish was a very special dog.

Nicola Ross (13)
The Community School of Auchterarder, Auchterarder

One Life

We've only got one life,
As far as I can see,
So why can't we live it
As we want it to be?
We don't all fit one mould,
We don't all look the same,
We need to be ourselves,
And not feel any shame.

If our face, it doesn't fit,
Or our bodies look wrong,
If our clothes lack certain design,
Don't sing the same old song.

We've only got one life,
As far as I can see.
So why can't we live it,
As we want it to be?
If our skin is white,
Or if our skin is black,
Why do we feel the need, to constantly attack?

We don't all hold the same belief,
Why can't we see what lies beneath?
Why can't we accept,
That life holds no grand plan,
Except to be kinder to our fellow man?

We've only got one life,
As far as I can see,
So I plan to live it
As I want it to be.

I plan to laugh,
I plan to cry,
I plan to spread my wings and fly.
I plan to see what lies beneath,
Discover other people's belief,
Then I can say, hand on heart,
For the whole wide world to see,
I lived my entire life,
As I wanted it to be!

Natalie Richardson (14)
The Compton School, London

Let Me See!
(From psychiatrist to student)

Show me your eyes
I just want to see
Please, open your eyes
And smile at me.

I feel for you
Deep down in my soul
I just want to leap out
And accomplish every goal.

Open up,
Just let me see
What's inside you
And, what's inside me.

I feel for you
Deep down in my soul,
I just want to leap out
And accomplish every goal.

Benjamin Tinslay (13)
The Compton School, London

Protest Poem

In times, long past,
Our ancestors would sit
Around a piano to pass the time.
In an age that's closer
Came the radio;
The wonderful speaking box.
Now, however,
In this modern era
We are, all of us, staring at garbage
On a new little gadget named telly!

It seemed a miracle when it first hit the shops,
At last, it seemed we could see!
But slowly and surely,
Over many a year,
Excrement crept on TV!

I don't know who allowed it,
I don't know why it is there,
But suddenly 'Big Brother' was on the air!
What a great idea! Now, finally,
We can now sit down and watch people . . .
Doing very little!

Of course the Big B is on Channel 4,
It is expected to be poor.
At least the BBC is cool.
Well that was true,
Until Miss Robinson appeared.
For a month or two,
Her wink was number one
Why's it still here?
Every day! Always the same!
Surely its only viewers
Are only checking to see
If 'The Simpsons' are on
(Which, by the way, has gone!)

Thanks to the television,
Most of the western world
Think George Orwell copied Davina McCall
(If they've even heard of '1984'!)
Thanks to television,
Our main ambassador to America
Is a wrinkled redhead who can't smile!

Television? Bah!

Edward Reade Banham (15)
The Compton School, London

Grandpa To Grandson

Trust me son:
Life is like a see-saw going up and down till it stops.
Not seeing your mum, no more cuddling you all around,
Life for you is not like mine, you're always enjoying life
And it's sound fine,
But for me it is just a big frown waiting for my life to die down.

This is where the pain hurts,
from my head to my very foot.
The days are getting shorter while your life is going quicker.
I just know the Earth don't need me no more,
Especially as I can't do much more.
As the days fade out I grow weaker and weaker,
My heart starts to slow down, till it has done its job,
So has my body as it stands still like a snowman,
Going nowhere, but melting on the spot.
That is why I tell you son, life is like a see-saw
Going up and down till it stops.

Karl Jackson
The Compton School, London

Boredom

I'm bored
There's nothing to do
Nothing
Not a sausage

Daytime TV is rubbish
And morning
And evening
In fact *all* TV is rubbish and boring
Boring, boring, boring

My friends are all away
Maybe when my brother comes home
We could play a game
Like Scrabble or Monopoly
But they're all boring,
Boring, boring, boring

The clock's ticking
The tap's dripping
The boiler's clanging
Maybe it's broken
I could fix it!
That would be something to do
But that's too hard
And boring
Even more boring than games or TV
Boring, boring, boring

I could read
Or write a story
Or draw a picture
But they're all boring
Boring, boring, boring

People say boredom is a state of mind
But they're wrong
It's where you are
And who you're with
And what you're doing
Not what you *choose* to do with your time

All this boredom
It makes my brain ache
I hate this moment
It's so boring
Boring, boring, boring.

Olivia Katis (13)
The Compton School, London

Year 7 To A Year 3

Life is like a galloping horse
Running down the race course.
You're having fun when you're seven
Before you know it you're eleven.

The most important thing was play
Now you have to work all day.
Big decisions have to be made
If you are going to make the grade.

Be prepared for the future to come
You'll write so much you'll have a sore thumb.
There will be hard work at school and at home
Friends will help you out so you won't be alone.

There are going to be obstacles in your way
But don't worry, it will be OK.
Life was fun when I was young
But real life has just begun.

Adam Nikpour (12)
The Compton School, London

Sergeant To Soldier

Well soldier, I'll tell you
Life isn't a machine gun
With fake bullets in it,
Or with still triggers,
It's like a one metre long
Flexible ruler
I will tell you why I called it that
Well, when it's made, you are born
When snapped, you are dead
It's flexible because
You have a different mood
Like if you are angry
You fight for freedom,
If you are happy
You fight bravely,
So it means you die.
So I hope you learnt a lesson, boys,
And to be honest,
Life for me ain't been no one metre flexible ruler.

Nicholas Nicolaou (12)
The Compton School, London

About School

I love to learn at school each day
I nearly always do what my teachers say
I do my best when there is work to do
And I like to show off to you
I help my friends
I love to share
'Cause I'm the kid who really cares
But it's not always about school
But what I do
Even a story is a special thing.
The ones that I have read,
They do not stay inside the books,
They stay inside my head
I saw my last year's teacher.
I thought *has she shrunk an inch or two?*
It took me time to figure,
She was no shorter;
I'd just grown.

And that's a fact
See what school does to you!
Makes you lose your mind too!

Halima Mohammed (14)
The Compton School, London

Prejudiced People

I see prejudiced people as small-minded,
not quite clever enough to see,
that if everyone was the same as them,
what a boring place the world would be.
Think before you discriminate,
don't judge a book by its cover,
inside there are countless possibilities,
and so much we can learn from each other.
It's great that everyone's different,
get to know people before you judge,
overlook their creed or colour of skin,
before you hold your grudge.
Racists and homophobes p*** me off
and those who judge the disabled, too,
in their case, they didn't get to choose who they are,
but think, it's not too late for you!
There's still time for you to open your mind,
to forget your opinions and prejudices.

Let's all think before we stick labels on others,
think how much easier life would be,
if we put our prejudices behind us,
and joined hands in unity!

Jo Taylor (14)
The Compton School, London

The Environment

Everywhere I look the environment is being destroyed
Rivers are polluted
Trees are damaged.
Where grass once lay
Now lives a seven-storey building.
As autumn leaves fall trees are slaughtered
As the dying flowers wither
Trees are being turned into paper.
Whales, dolphins and sea birds
Drown in toxic waste dumped at sea
And die covered with oil
Caused by spills.
As the day turns to dusk
Stars can't be seen
As a thick layer of chemicals over the night
Scenery only allowing glimpse
Of the bright light to show
But this is only if we are lucky.
As the sun rises, people rise with it
Allowing once again another day
Of
Slaughter, torture, distraction and devastation.
For everything we gain, the environment
Loses much, much more.

Gemini Tailor (14)
The Compton School, London

Slavery Poem

'What is slavery?' you say
Slavery is imprisonment
Slavery is suffering
Slavery is death
In the end.

'What is slavery?' you say
Slavery is contrast
Slavery is work
Slavery is what separates the weak
From the powerful.
It is what creates hatred
Between people.
It is when people are treated
Like animals.
Slaves have to do whatever they
Are commanded to do.

'What is slavery?' you say
It is when people do what they are
Told to do
When people are not free
When people are treated unfairly
When people don't get respect
When people are forced to do things
They wish not to do.

The world 'slave'
And the word 'lifeless'
Do you see any difference?
Neither do I.

Tejas Depala (15)
The Compton School, London

A Life Story

Life is a story,
Complex or simple,
Surprising or dull,
Average or extreme.

Life is a story,
Each page a new wonder,
Cheetah's speed or snail's pace . . .
Depending on the tone,
Exciting and speedy,
But if it's boring
And slow,
You have to read it *again* . . .
And *again* . . .
And *again*.

Life is a story,
Different from each other,
Subtly or hugely,
Discreetly or unnoticeably.

Life is a story,
About a girl or boy,
A man or a woman,
A parent or a child.

Life is a story,
You don't know what will happen next . . .
Until you read on . . .
One page after another,
Just like this poem.

Life is a story,
With a happy or sad ending,
I hope mine is happy,
But what will yours be?

Jessica Sofizade (12)
The Compton School, London

Please Save Me!

Raiding, fighting, bombing, shooting,
Some are killing whilst most are dying,
Tonnes of bombs blow every day.
There is no escape, can't even play

Red-coloured rocks around me,
All from people just like me.
There is no hope, just have to be.
Why don't they stop? Please save me.

Rifles, ships, bullets and missiles.
All day long, just cry of whistles
Children screaming, babies crying,
All night long, hysterical yelling.

Red-coloured rocks around me,
All from people just like me.
There is no hope, just have to be.
Why don't they stop? Please save me.

The town went on weeping,
All through the war.
Soldiers showed no shame.
Just fell to the floor.

Red-coloured rocks around me,
All from people just like me.
There is no hope, just have to be.
Why don't they stop? Please save me.

Fear and pain on the battlefield.
Blood and sweat all over the shield.

Red-coloured rocks around me,
All from people just like me.
There is no hope, just have to be.
Why don't they stop? Please save me!

Kayan Poon (14)
The Compton School, London

Stand Out

Perfect teeth, silky hair,
Perfect figure, complexion fair.
Skirts contrasting, white and black,
Trousers ironed, designer backpack.
Expensive shoes, sparkly earrings worn,
Everything to perfection, nothing dirty or torn.

Break time comes, children play,
Groups close together, all have their say.
Glances over shoulders at the unwanted friend,
The outcast of the year, left alone to fend.
Whispers stir and rumours spread,
Only takes one comment for the lies to imbed.

'Tatty uniform, she's different from us,
I don't like the way she looks,
She'll never earn my trust. She's the new kid,
She's different, let's just ignore her or, even better,
I've got a rumour to stir.'

It spreads like wildfire, circles around,
But she sits there all day, without making a sound,
But slowly inside, her heart is breaking,
This is the third school they've tried and she's sick of her
                                        soul aching.

Hit, pushed over, insults thrown,
Surrounded by bullies or sitting on her own.
Never lived in a house, couldn't afford
To have the luxuries of a TV, couch or a Ford.
So labelled she was, along with others,
Ones with no mothers, fathers, half-brothers.
Different accents, clothes not as clean,
Don't have much money for food, so quite skinny and lean.

The children will taunt, they'll stare and they'll yell,
But as the bullying will worsen they'll never ever tell.

Carole Walsh
The Compton School, London

Under Fire

We're stuck in a trench or a crater,
There are shells bombarding all over us,
All there is, is a black sky and fire,
We have no idea where it's coming from,
Or where to run.
The other day I had my pay,
I saw my friend blown away!
As I watched I had bullets flying from all angles,
I stayed low, crawled up and out,
I started to gasp,
I started to grind,
I don't know why I might have been blind.
I didn't mention a bullet was close to my ear.
All I had was my Lee Enfield custom rifle,
A radio strapped to my back,
I ran back to call for help,
We didn't know what to call for,
Then someone bellowed, 'Air support,
Maybe the cruisers!'
What we saw was fireworks,
Bombs went off and blazes of fire,
We heard cries of death and pain,
'Use your bayonet!' was the order,
The war was won,
We were the victors,
We had shots of Bacardi rum to our victory.
In the morning we shipped out,
Ready for our next orders and mission,
Under fire.

Calvin Ellis (15)
Wansdyke Special School, Bath

Ode To The Stream At Bellies Brae Car Park (In Kirriemuir)

I walk past the car park which gleams metallic rainbows
Of vehicles that appear in all colours and sizes and shapes.
The ground is slick with two hour old rain
The blackened earth seeming to weep in pain
Of this new gravel mask it is forced to wear forever.

I jump past the miniature slope, daring my mind
But I graze my knees as I land and now it stings for a while.
Another new wound to add to my collection
Of the times I've fallen in my life,
Yet something near me has worse wounds.

The steam that runs under the small bridge
Under the wooden slanted planks
Like a submissive prisoner below the decks of a ship.
This stream is not even a river yet,
But I fear it will not live long enough for that.

Beer cans give it aluminium bruises as the flowing water must divert
Around the new wounds it obtains.
Plastic bags trap water, suffocating the baby stream
All the bag does is act as a body bag for the unfortunate,
The unfortunate stream and any poor creature still in it.

Once upon a time, this stream had life in it
Now it is nothing more than a garbage pit
It is in the shape of a trench-like trough
Perhaps to reflect the pigheadedness of the litterbugs.
It's a crying shame, but the stream has enough tears.

So this stream I see usually four times a week
Has never before looked so meek.
I wished that we looked after it better
But then I remember one thing.
A broken stream is the same as a broken dream.
No one cares about either.

Arran Middleton (17)
Websters High School, Kirriemuir

Forever Flowing

It flows,
  Soundlessly
    Slowly
      Surely.
        Slipping
      Through silver,
    Glistening
  Gliding
Never ceasing

It swims,
  Quietly
    quickly
      Cautiously.
        Riding
      Through waves,
    Rippling
  Reflecting
Never relenting

It surges,
  Lonely
    Longingly
      Lustfully.
        Crashing
      Through coral,
    Floating
  Flying
    Forever beginning.

Emma Craddock (14)
Websters High School, Kirriemuir

Needles

Searching for
A decent vein
Taking
Time
Don't
Complain
Filling it up with
Strange liquid
Five mls, ten mls,
Fifteen then twenty
The point looks like a
Horrible ugly claw
Is she? Isn't she?
It is going to hurt.
I
N
I
T
G
O
E
S
!

Alex Hackett (14)
Wilson Stuart Special School, Erdington

Linh's Lovely Lines

Victorious Victoria is very vain,
Abominable Ann always ambles around school,
Horrible Helena hops home,
Crazy Kelly is cute and clean,
Terrific Mrs Tomkinson teases terrified tots,
Terrible Mr Totty teaches tortuous times tables.

Linh Hoang (15)
Wilson Stuart Special School, Erdington

After School

Ring the doorbell (point finger),
Into the house (walking action with fingers),
Take off your coat (pretend to take off your coat)
And throw down your bag (pretend to throw bag on the floor).

Hello Mum (wave)
Hello Dad (wave),
Stroke the cat (stroking action),
And pat the dog (patting action).

Rush into the kitchen (walking action with fingers),
Grab some food (grab with two hands),
Drink a bottle of pop (drinking action),
Go out to play (walking action with fingers).

Come in, it's cold (hug yourself),
Watch the TV (stare ahead),
Go up the stairs (climbing action with hands),
Listen to the music (make headphones over ears with hands).

Wash your face (pretend to wash your face),
Brush your teeth (pretend to brush your teeth),
Play with the PlayStation (play on imaginary PlayStation),
Jump into bed (move arms forward),
And snore off your head (lie back in chair and pretend to be asleep).

Adrian Holloway, Kenetia Thompson & Joe Spence (14)
Wilson Stuart Special School, Erdington

Rosie Rabbit

Her fur is a fluffy white cloud of cotton wool,
Her eyes are pale pink rosebuds,
Her nose is a sneeze itching to come out.
She is a kangaroo hopping in a field.
She is a tiny mouse squeaking.
Her teeth are a machine chomping up her food.
Her ears are aerials picking up sound waves.
She's a mountaineer clambering up the furniture.

Katy Evans (14)
Wilson Stuart Special School, Erdington

At The Zoo

Watch the monkeys
Peeling some bananas.
Listen to the tigers
Roaring very loud.

Huge, giant elephants
Stomping on the ground,
The hissing long snakes
Slithering round and round.

The jolly, jumping kangaroos
With babies in their pouch,
The long-legged giraffes
Reaching up the tree.

See the peckish penguins
Waddling round the pool,
The dizzy dolphins diving,
Splashing water everywhere.

I am just happy to be me
Watching all the animals
On this sunny day.

Callum Mucklow & Laura Tomlinson (14)
Wilson Stuart Special School, Erdington

Snow

Snow
Snow falls
Snow is here
Snow is melting
Snow is on the ground
Snow is freezing all day
Snow is blowing very fast
I put my coat on and go out
I build a snowman very quickly.

Gurdeep Kainth (13)
Wilson Stuart Special School, Erdington

A Day In The Classroom With 8.1

Active Alex laughs at Terrible Totty.
He tries to torture her with the two times table.

Annoying Asifa squeaks and screams at Terrible Totty.
'Silence, you simpleton!' shouted shrieking Totty.

Toni tried to take Nathan and run to the car park
For a quick kiss and cuddle.

They were swiftly spotted by tall Totty,
Who threw threes at them.

Devious Dean dives under the desk to escape evil work.
He silently steals Miss Simpson's shiny shoe
And leaves her hopping home.

Zubair Rehman (14)
Wilson Stuart Special School, Erdington

Love Is In The Air!

Love is many things,
It is feeling cared for by your boyfriend,
It is holding hands, cuddling and kissing,
It is feeling safe enough to tell each other
Your deepest secrets.
It makes you feel warm-hearted,
It gives you butterflies in your tummy
When you kiss your boyfriend.
It makes your boyfriend
Feel part of your family.

Toni Bird (14)
Wilson Stuart Special School, Erdington

A Day In School With 10.2

Daring Dominique dashes down the corridor to dinner
Followed by lazy Linh who loves luscious lips and
Listening to loud, lousy Blazin' Squad music.
Around the corner amazing Ann is awake and always active.
Jolly, joking Jason jokes with Jade.
Adorable Anisah amazes us in assembly.
Troublesome Mr Totty teaches us times tables
Time and time again, *too tough* for us.
Big, bossy Mr Buxton blows up the Bunsen burners
In the science laboratory.
Brilliant.

Victoria Bates (15)
Wilson Stuart Special School, Erdington

My Wheelchair

My glowing, blue and black
Wheelchair is super fast,
With a golf ball control
It has soft, comfortable seating.
it gives me freedom
And independence,
It helps me speed to meet the
Love of my life.
I whizz down the corridor
To my next lesson.
Zoom!

Nathan Green (14)
Wilson Stuart Special School, Erdington

Lunchtime At Wilson Stuart School

It's lunchtime and lovely Linh loves
His lunch laughing with delightful Dom
Who devours her dinner.
Likeable Lee giggles and gossips about girls.
Active Anisah asks me about my auntie.
Munching Melissa eating a melon
Muttering about her friend Dominique
Animated Alex arrives late for lunch.
She piles her plate with peas and pizza.
Auntie Ann eats her apple, always ready to help and humour us.
Singing Miss Simpson shuffles her shoes as she grooves on down.
The bell goes and it's time for registration.

Dominique Levy (16)
Wilson Stuart Special School, Erdington

Sad Is A Grey Word

Sad is a grey word,
As dull as a cloudy sky,
As tearful as an upset child,
As flat as a pancake,
As empty as an empty room,
As tasteless as nothing,
As stale as a loaf of old bread,
As sluggish as a worm,
As sad as a tiger in the zoo,
As still as death.

Mithun Soul (13)
Wilson Stuart Special School, Erdington

Happy Is A Yellow Word

Happy is a yellow word,
As cheerful as someone's birthday,
As bright as a sunny day,
As eager as a little girl starting school,
As joyful as a bouncy ball,
As smiley as a funny clown,
As sweet as chocolate cake,
As silky as pyjamas,
As infectious as giggling,
As merry as a little giggling girl.

Jade Hinsley (12)
Wilson Stuart Special School, Erdington

Young Is A Pink Word

Young is a pink word,
As bouncy as a trampoline,
As new as a shiny coin,
As fluffy as a kitten,
As innocent as a newborn baby,
As chubby as baby's cheeks,
As chewy as gristle,
As lively as a football match,
As playful as a puppy,
As happy as a clown.
Young is a pink word.

Kirsty Turner (13)
Wilson Stuart Special School, Erdington

Aeroplane

I fly through the air
Like a bird without a care.
I'm a big piece of metal
With a nose, wing and tail.
I fly through all weathers,
Including rain, thunder and hail.
Carrying people over the sea and land,
Taking them to exciting new places,
Such as mountains, cities and sand.
At take-off, motors spinning round and round,
Engine roars and buzzes,
Lifting passengers off the ground.

Saad Ashraf (14)
Wilson Stuart Special School, Erdington

Tongue Twisters

Happy Helena helps horses.
Daft Darren drives a car.
Aggressive Ann always attacks.
Horrible Mr Hughes hollers in the hall.
Cute Kelly keeps giving Jason a kiss.
Racing Mrs Rowland rides down the road.
Trusty Mrs Tomkinson teaches terrible tricks.
Singing Miss Simpson sings silly songs.
Bossy Mr Buxton bashes boys.
Wise Mr White whittles away at his wood.

Jason Micklewright (15)
Wilson Stuart Special School, Erdington